I0007832

SQL for Beg

The Practice Guide to Learn SQL in 1 Day
+ 10 Tips +Exercises, Projects &
Applications

By James Deep

Table of Contents

Introduction 1

Chapter 1: An Introduction to SQL 3

Structured Query Language (SQL) 4

Benefits of Working with Databases 5

Types of Structured Query Language Commands 7

Chapter 2: SQL Commands 11

Select 11

Update 12

Delete 13

Insert 13

Create Table 14

Alter Table 14

Drop Table 15

Create Index & Drop Index 15

Create View 15

Group By 16

Join 16

Create Database and Alter Database 17

Other SQL Commands 17

Chapter 3: Creating Your First Database And Table .. 19

Steps 20

Creating Your First Database and Table Using Command Line 25

Table of Contents

Introduction 1

Chapter 1: An Introduction to SQL 3

Structured Query Language (SQL) 4

Benefits of Working with Databases 5

Types of Structured Query Language Commands................. 7

Chapter 2: SQL Commands 11

Select 11

Update.. 12

Delete.. 13

Insert 13

Create Table 14

Alter Table... 14

Drop Table 15

Create Index & Drop Index 15

Create View...15

Group By 16

Join.. 16

Create Database and Alter Database 17

Other SQL Commands..17

Chapter 3: Creating Your First Database And Table .. 19

Steps 20

Creating Your First Database and Table Using Command Line... 25

Chapter 4: Inserting, Updating And Deleting Data 27

Inserting, Updating, and Deleting Data *31*

SQL Update Multiple Columns *37*

Deleting Data from SQL Table *38*

Chapter 5: Modifying And Controlling Tables 39

.... *39*

Changing Tables *39*

Modifying and Removing Constraints *44*

Chapter 6: Working With Subqueries 45

The SQL Server Subquery *47*

Creating New Databases in SQL Programming *49*

Industries That Use SQL Programming *50*

Common SQL Database Systems *51*

The Relevance of the Database System to Social Networks..52

Chapter 7: Combining Queries 54

How to Create Union Query by Creating and Uniting the Select Queries *56*

An Example You Can Recreate the Northwind Sample Database *59*

Chapter 8: SQL Mathematics And Statistics 62

Mathematics and Statistics for Data Science *63*

Chapter 9: Saving Time With Views, Functions, And Triggers 73

Best Practices and Approach for One to Achieve a Goal *73*

Database Objects 75

Chapter 10: SQL Embedded Java Program 80

Overview of SQL 81

Benefits of Java Programming 84

Benefits of SQL 86

Disadvantages of SQLJ Programming 87

Requirements for SQLJ 88

Development Goals of SQLJ 88

Chapter 11: Common Rookie Mistakes 90

Chapter 12: Built-In Functions & Calculations 98

Types of SQL Functions 98

Categories of Functions 100

SQL Calculations 102

The Importance of SQL Built-In Functions and Mathematical
Applications 103

Downsides of In-Built Functions 105

Chapter 13: SQL Joins 107

How to Setup the Database Environment in SQL 108

Basics of SQL Joins 109

Types of SQL Joins 110

Chapter 14: Ten Tips For Easy Retrieval 114

Chapter 15: Stored Routines And Variables 123

Declaring the Variables 124

Chapter 16: Exercises, Projects And Applications 129

Examples of Exercises in SQL...*130*

Projects in SQL Programming *132*

Applications of SQL...*133*

Conclusion 139

Introduction

Computer languages have become more popular today since the introduction of instructions fed into machines. As almost everything now become more reliant on computers, hence is the need to learn a few things, including understanding computer SQL programming language.

The following chapters will discuss SQL programming, which is among one of the many programming languages out there. As learning the basics is critical in every course, the book highlights the fundamental essential components of SQL programming. As such, you will learn about the introduction of how to get started, including the primary definition and reasons why it is crucial. SQL programming also entails various benefits and types which will learn. Besides, the chapters provide a quick overview of server and client technology, which is also essential while learning SQL programming.

That said, learning about the introduction part puts you at the forefront of meeting your goals when taking a lesson in SQL programming. Therefore, the chapters will also discuss the basic commands commonly used.

Like other programming languages, SQL programming encompasses different commands, but in this case, this book will solely focus on the basic ones to bring out the general idea.

After having the necessary preparations, you will also learn about how to create your initial database as well as tables. It is also essential to learn how to put the lesson learned into practice to ascertain its applicability in the computer industry.

Chapter 1: An Introduction to SQL

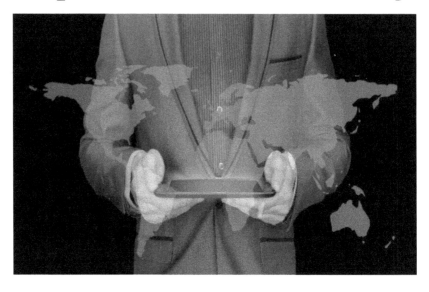

Structured Query Language or SQL primarily deals with databases crucial for developers, analysts, and administrators essential for providing skills on how to create room to store data in an organized manner. Learning SQL can sometimes become challenging, especially when you fail to commit adequate time as well as taking inappropriate approaches. However, learning SQL programming will significantly promote careers in SQL, as it is one of the most demanded skills globally today. You should understand that learning about SQL programming without practical is usually a failing course.

SQL was first introduced by Ted Code but later enhanced by Donald D. Chamberlin and Raymond F. Boyce in the early 1970s. The initial language name was referred to as SEQUEL,

Structured English Query Language, and incorporated to help in information retrieval. The name was later changed to SQL and first used commercially in 1979 and the subsequent years. Over the years, its development continued leading to the introduction of more advanced SQL commands. By 1990, there existed new versions with standard Database Language SQL with the recent version released in 2016. However, various developments and advanced have witnessed over time, making SQL programming flexible and more reliable, especially in storage and quick retrieval of information when the need arises.

Structured Query Language (SQL)

Structured Query Language or SQL is a standard programming tool commonly preferred by developers, analysts and administrators to design, create, and supervise rational databases. These databases comprise different sets of tables which entail rows or columns filled with data. On each column, the database or table is filled with information of a given set of identical data such as name, address, cost, or other values. On the other hand, rows usually contain data values that intersect the information of each column. Generally, databases are mostly full of tables containing data sets crucial for a given organization, including the storage of data for quick retrieval. Since it is among computer programming languages, SQL is a universal coding programming tool commonly considered a doorway to learn other programming languages such as Python.

It was first introduced in the 1970s, and learners do not necessarily require prior knowledge in programming to venture into learning SQL programming. When you are ready to learn about SQL, it is always advisable to understand the basics by beginning with simple queries before jumping into complex processes. Read and learn from different sources, including tutorials, while making progress each day. Besides, engage in creating and designing different databases to advance in trickier programming practices.

Benefits of Working with Databases

Ease of Access

A database typically accommodates massive amounts of data, which may include millions of specific data. For instance, when you use other forms of data storage units, retrieving such information may become a bit complicated due to the load in the system. However, SQL, like most databases, provides straightforward access to specific information. That is, you can readily search the needed data from millions of files and gain access to it in seconds. Besides, if employees of a given organization need to access the data from different regions or areas, all they need is a reliable internet connection and access to this information at any time. Therefore, employees can continue working with the data when traveling or at home.

Restrictions of Access

Databases are an essential tool for the storage of data, especially when you need to create a platform to secure a company or other sensitive information. This is because the databases have become more secure today, making it difficult for unauthorized personnel from accessing the data. However, this is offered in two ways; a user may access the data but only read rather than make changes while others may be able to read and make necessary changes. This is crucial, especially for employees and the management when sharing data vital for the running of the organization.

Self-Describing Capabilities

Database systems usually are fitted with adequate room to create and design tables with a complete description of each data stored. When, for instance, feeding a piece of given information into the system, the database will provide a summary of each set. Each dataset will have a description providing a separation of data which fit specific areas. This way, database systems are considered self-describing as they contain metadata descriptions essential for the identification of data and relations in different tables within a particular system.

Provision of Data Redundancy Controls

Databases commonly store each dataset in one place as an approach to promote data storage, especially when there is a need to create effective database systems. However, some instances of data redundancy may occur as a way to enhance the performance of the system. Databases primarily offer controls to data redundancy but controlled solely by the application. The general idea is to introduce as reduced redundancy as possible when creating and designing databases.

Allowance of Data Independency

Database management systems also accompany the benefit of data independence, which makes metadata and other data descriptions to become separate from the program. This process is made possible because data structures are handled separately by the system but not included in the program. More so, the database allows for transaction processing of data, which involves concurrency control subsystems. This, therefore, ensures that the data remains valid and similar when undergoing transaction processing.

Types of Structured Query Language Commands

Data Definition Language (DDL)

This is a command type that allows users to develop and restructure physical database structure, and when executed, it makes changes immediately. The most commonly used commands in this type include CREATE, ALTER and DROP TABLE, CREATE INDEX and CREATE VIEW, among others. These commands usually focus on the definition of the table more so during designing and making other changes to the database system in general.

Data Manipulation Language (DML)

This is the command where manipulation of values, objects, and figures within the table undergo changes, mainly when focusing on mistakes on the datasets. DML is often done when the table has been created, and a database designed by DDL commands. The commands used include INSERT, UPDATE, and DELETE. Besides, these commands are among the most beneficial, especially when making changes in the database management systems.

Data Control Language (DCL)

A data control command is an SQL command which allows users to access the information stored within the database system quickly. ALTER PASSWORD, GRANT, REVOKE, and CREATE SYNONYM are the commonly used commands essential for the management of data. Besides, DCL is also critical handling matters related to data control, including controlling the user to gain access to the database system accordingly.

Data Query Language (DQL)

This is an SQL query that comprises only one command but widely used today as it combines with other SQL functions to retrieve and collect data from specific tables under given parameters. The command SELECT works well with additional options and clauses of SQL and handles all queries, either simple or complex. Also, the Data Query Language command is applicable for vague and specific datasets.

Transactional Control Commands

As the name suggests, this command allows for the management of problems and queries involving transactions of data in any database system. Transaction Control Language is often used for making changes where the need is and uses both 'undo' and 'apply' options for making changes. The commands used include COMMIT, ROLLBACK, SAVEPOINT, and SET TRANSACTION. As such, making changes as well as modifications can be made without any significant complications when using commands in SQL programming.

Server and Client Technology

Server and client technology is an ability to separate specific functions of programs or applications into two or more parts, providing a relationship between computers. In other words, it is the ability of one program, the client, to make a request to two or more processors, the server, and they comply with the application. In this case, the client can access, present, and make modifications to this data from the main desktop computer. On the other hand, the server acts as a storage unit to supply protected data to the client. Therefore, server and client technology create a network structure where data can be retrieved with minimal stress, especially when there is a need to supply the needed information.

However, the interconnection arises where clients significantly rely on servers for supply or relevant components such as files and devices as well as processing capabilities. Servers, therefore, are compelling computer systems suitable for handling file servers in the form of disk drives, print, and network servers. Clients often work stations or PCs where applications are run. The model is usually through a computer network with an active and partitioned workload system on separated hardware. Despite so, clients do not share resources but communicates with the server for content or other service functions.

Chapter 2: SQL Commands

```
* @var boolean
*/
define('PSI_INTERNAL_XML', false);

if (version_compare("5.2", PHP_VERSION, ">")) {
    die("PHP 5.2 or greater is required!!!");
}
if (!extension_loaded("pcre")) {
    die("phpSysInfo requires the pcre extension to php in order to work
        properly.");
}

require_once APP_ROOT.'/includes/autoloader.inc.php';

// Load configuration
require_once APP_ROOT.'/config.php';

if (!defined('PSI_CONFIG_FILE') || !defined('PSI_DEBUG')) {
    $tpl = new Template("/templates/html/error_config.html");
    echo $tpl->fetch();
    die();
```

As mentioned earlier, SQL used specific commands which control the tables within database systems, especially when handling multiple tables with big data. Each table is often defined by a given name, such as customers or orders. It should be known that all functions or commands are done with SQL statements. More so, SQL statements, as well as keywords, are not case sensitive, and some databases may require semicolons on statements as a standard format. Therefore, SQL statements include SELECT, UPDATE, DELETE, INSERT INTO, and more.

Select

Like most computer commands, SELECT is primarily utilized for querying the database as well as in the retrieval of intended data that matches the parameters specified. For example,

SELECT *column1* [, *column2, …*], FROM *(table name)*, WHERE *(condition)*. When writing the SELECT command, you may use conditional clauses such as equal (=), greater than (>), less than (<), greater than or equal (>=), less than or equal (<), not equal to (<>) and LIKE. When you write SELECT * FROM (table_name), it readily returns the entire data from the table and may, at times, include quotes around the text. However, do not use quotes to enclose mathematical objects. When using LIKE, ensure it matches a pattern, especially when involving the use of (%), which denotes 0 in SQL programming. For example, 'A%' resembles all strings which use A as the first letter while '%a' matches data, which ends with a. Similarly, '%a%' matches strings or data which have an 'a' between values or information in a given table or database.

Update

When there are preexisting values in a table and there in need to change them, then the UPDATE command is used. The command uses the functions UPDATE *(table_name)*, SET *colX=valX* [, *colY=valY,…*], WHERE *(condition)*. This type of SQL command is applicable when there is a need to change, alter, or edit rows in a given table, therefore, creating a more significant process of the management of database systems. At some point, specific rows can be modified without causing any impact to data in a similar column.

Delete

As the name suggests, this is a term used in computing for the removal of unwanted, repeated, or unused data from the system. Similarly, SQL also utilizes a similar function as a command to remove unwanted records from a given table within the system. In this case, it uses the feature DELETE FROM (table_name), WHERE (*conditions*), and the file will be deleted successfully. You can also clear the entire information without getting rid of the table using the function DELETE * FROM (*table_name*). Therefore, when removing the record, the specified range or conditions set determines the extent of what you are getting rid of. However, some conditions may compromise the data if you delete vital data due to wrongly and unspecified parameters.

Insert

When the table has been created, that is, the columns and rows are specified as required, data is then fed into the system. However, it is usually challenging to feed information one at a time in each column and row more so when the data is bulky. This may result in errors that may go unnoticed, therefore compromising the future. Therefore, SQL uses the INSERT VALUE, also referred to as the INSERT INTO command, to feed data into the table and at required columns and rows. The programming language uses the function INSERT INTO (*table_name*), (col1,........., coln), VALUES (val1,....,valn) to insert values. The 'n' denotes the number of the last column in your table where the previous value will be added. In this case, inserting the values into the table becomes straightforward, quicker and prevents cases emerging from sparse data entry formats.

Create Table

The CREATE TABLE clause is another basic command of SQL essential for developing a table to insert the information needed. The function used is CREATE TABLE (*table_name), (column1 data type, column2 data type, column3 data type,...)*. When creating a table, there are also other considerations, which include char for which the fixed-length character string, varchar also size, number with a maximum column value and data value. As database systems comprise of several tables, you can add more tables in a certain database and insert your values.

Alter Table

In some cases, you may have created a table with either more or fewer columns hence the need to delete or add. Therefore, SQL provides a query that enables you to quickly remove or columns to an existing table by first specifying a data type along with the number of columns to add or delete. The format used in this case is ALTER TABLE (table_name), DROP COLUMN colname. That is, specify the table name in which you are to add or delete columns and then set the parameters for which data type and on which column you wish to modify.

Drop Table

Another necessary command used in SQL is for getting rid of the entire table from the database when it is unwanted of there is a need to create a new one. That is, SQL allows you to use the command DELETE * FROM (*table_name)* and drop a given table. As a basic command in SQL, DROP TABLE is crucial, especially when you want to have another table with fresh details, which differs significantly when compared to the previous one.

Create Index & Drop Index

Another typical command in SQL is for creating indexes also essential in databases. When you want to create an index, it involves developing a search key that facilitates the process of searching and retrieving data quickly. Like the DROP TABLE command, DROP INDEX means deleting of an existing index from the database and the development of a new one.

Create View

As a result of an SQL SELECT, CREATE VIEW is another command or query that entails a virtual table but with fields from more than one table in a database system. As it has similar values like that of the original table, view tables are meant to provide a preview of the information stored in one or more tables within a database. Therefore, a view or virtual table can be considered a real table. The function used is CREATE TABLE view_name AS, SELECT col_name(s), FROM table_name, WHERE *(condition)*. View table can be utilized within a command, saved procedures, and from other similar commands. As such, this facilitates the process of adding more functions and linking them, therefore, presenting the necessary data to the user.

Group By

The GROUP BY is a much newer command added to facilitate the process of grouping aggregate results searched by column values. In other words, GROUP BY entails enabling the database to group data with respect to the similarities highlighted by the user into a given column. The format used included; SELECT col_name, function (col_name) FROM table_name GROUP BY col_name. However, the 'WHERE' keyword was replaced in this command with 'HAVING,' which brings out the condition. Therefore, the function used is SELECT col_name, function (col_name) FROM table_name, GROUP BY col_name, HAVING function (col_name) conditions data. In this case, the user is, therefore, capable of grouping columns according to their requirements.

Join

Data may be spread among different tables within a single database; hence, you wish to collate these data into one table. Tables under a single database typically have a connection through the keys, therefore, making it easy to associate the data between different tables. As such, the tables can be linked together through the process of join in SQL programming. For example, if you have three tables with a connection such as customers, orders, and product supply, then you can join them using the JOIN command. As such, use the command SELECT customer_name, product name, FROM customer_name, order, product supply, WHERE customer = orders = product supply. Besides, the command also allows for INNER JOIN for the selection of two tables and LEFT JOIN to return all the rows to the initial table.

Create Database and Alter Database

When using the SQL programming tool, you may choose to create more than one database using the necessary command of CREATE DATABASE. The command quickly incorporates a fresh database where an individual can develop and design several tables within. Most often, you may create a database and then go ahead to make changes and modify the tables as well. As to modify the SQL database, you may use the statement ALTER DATABASE which readily modifies the system.

Other SQL Commands

ORDER BY is another clause that orders column names according to user needs using the command ORDER BY *col_name ASC* for ascending and *DESC* for descending. There is also IN, AND/OR, BETWEEN and AND. All these functions are essential for operating values in the table. For instance, IN is crucial for returning for a known value using the format SELECT * FROM *table_name* WHERE *col_name* IN *(val1, val2,...)*. BETWEEN and AND are vital for providing a range between two values and use the function SELECT * FROM *table_name* WHERE *col_name* BETWEEN *val1* AND *val2*. AND/OR may be used to join two or more values or conditions and uses either WHERE, AND, and OR formats to determine its viability.

Chapter 3: Creating Your First Database And Table

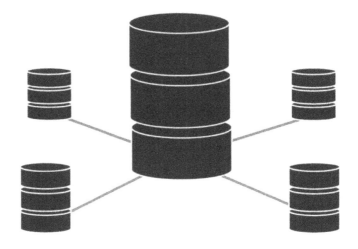

Before having a successful database with practical tables in SQL programming, both the creation of a database and then a table is required. However, there are several SQL data application software out there, but all have almost a similar step of creating a new database and tables. When you create your first database system, you will then have to design a table where you will feed your data and store it more securely and effectively. SQL offers a free graphical user interface, and it is easy to create.

The following is a step by step guide on how to create your first SQL database and tables before thinking of feeding your data.

Steps

Step 1: SQL Server Management Studio Software Installation

The firsts step in creating your first database and table is by acquiring the SQL software available for free online from Microsoft. This software comes fully packed, allowing you to interact and manage the SQL server with limited command-line instructions. Besides, it is crucial when it comes to using databases when in remote regions. Mac users can, however, utilize open-source programs, for instance, SQuirrel SQL, to maneuver through the Database system.

Step 2: Launch the SQL Studio

When you launch the SQL studio, the software occasionally requests a server at first that you will prefer using or the one you are using presently. If you have an already existing one, you may choose to input the permissions, authenticate, and connect. Some may prefer local database systems by setting a new name authenticate using a preferred name or address. Launching the SQL server management studio begins the process of interacting with the software and a path to creating your first database and table.

Step 3: Identify Database Folder

Immediately after the connection is made on either the local or remote, a Window will open on the left of the screen. On top, there will be a server where it will connect to. If not, you may click on the icon '+,' which will display multiple elements, including the option to create a new database. In some versions, you may see the icon for creating a new database immediately on the left drop-down Window. You can then click on 'Create New Database.'

Step 4: Create a New Database

As mentioned in step 3, the drop-down menu will fully display multiple options, including the one to create a new database. First, you will configure the database according to your parameters as well as providing the name for ease of identification. Most users prefer leaving the settings in their default, but you can change them if you are familiar with how they impact your process of data storage in the system. Note that when you create the database name, two files will generate the data automatically and log files. Data files are responsible for the storage of data while log files track all the changes, modifications, and other alterations made in the database.

Step 5: Create Your Tables

Databases often do not store data unless structures in forms of rows and tables are created for that data to remain organized. Tables are the primary storage units where data is held, but initially, you have to create the table before you insert the information. Similar to creating a new database, tables are also straightforward when creating. In the Databases folder, expand the Window then right-click on Tables and choose 'Nee Table.' Windows will open, displaying a table that can be easily manipulated towards the number rows and columns, titles, and how you want to organize your work. In this step, you will succeed in creating both the database and table, therefore, moving forward in organizing your task.

Step 6: Developing the Primary Key

The primary key plays a significant role in databases as it acts as a record number or ID for easy identification and remembrance when you view the page later. As such, it highly recommended creating these keys in the first column. There are many ways to do this and include entering the ID in the column field by typing *int* and deselecting the 'Allow Nulls.' Select the key icon found in the toolbar and marks it as the Primary key.

Step 7: Structure the Tables

Tables typically have multiple columns, also referred to as fields, and each column represents one element of data entries. When creating your table, you initially structured it to fit the number of data entries, therefore essential for each dataset as other primary keys. Thus, the structuring process will entail identifying each column with a given set of data. For example, FirstName column, Last name, and address column, among others.

Step 8: Creating Other Columns

Immediately you create the columns for primary keys; you will notice that there appear more columns below it. These are not for primary keys but essential for the insertion of other information. As such, ensure you input the correct data for each column to avoid filling the table with the wrong information. In the column, you will enter the 'nchar,' which is a data type for text, 'int' used for whole numbers, and 'decimal' for storage of decimal numbers.

Step 9: Saving the Table

After you finish creating the content in each field, you will notice that your table will consist of rows and columns. However, you will need to first save the table before entering the information. This can be done by selecting the Save icon also in the toolbar and name your table. When naming your table, ensure that you create a name that you can easily relate to the content or recognize. Besides, databases with different tables should have different names so that they can be identified easily.

Step 10: Add Data

Once the table is saved, you can now add the data into the system feeding each field with relevant information. However, you can confirm if the table is saved by expanding the Tables Folder and try to see if our table name is listed. If not, use the Table Folder to refresh the tables, and you will see your table. Back in the table, Right-click on the table where a drop dialog box will appear and select 'Edit Top 200 Rows'. The Window will then display fields for you to add data but ignore the primary keys as they will fill automatically. Continue with the same process until when you enter the last data in the table.

Step 11: Running the Table

After you have finished working on the table, you are to save the content so that you do not lose your work. As the table is already saved, click on 'Execute SQL' on the toolbar when you have finished entering data, and it will execute the process of feeding each data you entered into the columns. The parsing process may take a few seconds, depending on a load of data. If there are any errors in the feeding process, the system will show you where you input data incorrectly. More so, you can execute the program parsing of all the data by using the combination of 'ctrl' and 'R.'

Step 12: Data Querying

At this step, you have created your first database and table and successfully saved the information through SQL language programming. The database is now fully functional, and you henceforth create more tables within a single database. However, there is a limit on how many tables per database, but many users do not worry about this rule. You can, therefore, create new database systems you want and create more tables. At this end, you can query your data for reports or any relevant purposes, such as organizational or administrative purposes.

Often, having a general idea of SQL programming, especially for putting it into practice in creating databases and tables, allows you to advance your learning skills.

Creating Your First Database and Table Using Command Line

As already discussed in the last chapter, you can as well use SQL commands and statements to create databases and tables. The same applies to SQL Server Management Studio like the above guide, but commands and statements are used to give instructions to the system to perform a given function. As to build your first database, you use the command' SELECT DATABASE (*database_name)'* and hitting the execute button to create the program. The message on the screen should, therefore, be 'Command(s) completed successfully," showing that your database has been created.

As to use the database, run the command 'USE (*database_name),'* which tells the query window to run the new database program. On the other hand, creating a new table entails running the command 'CREATE TABLE (*table_name).'* Entering data follows the command 'INSERT DATA INTO (*table_name),* VALUES (table_name),' and repeating the same process for all the datasets you have. The same also allows for viewing the data you saved and includes the command format 'SELECT * FROM (table_name). All the above commands are the critical ones when it comes to maneuvering through different SQL databases. As such, it is always essential to learn about each SQL basic commands to execute programs readily.

Chapter 4: Inserting, Updating And Deleting Data

There is too much buzz available in the technological world about data. However, raw data is not so useful when on its own. SQL is pronounced as "sequel". It stands for Structured Query Language. It is typically a language that allows for communication through databases. This happens so that it can easily manage all the data contained within the databases.

In modern days, most businesses, both small and large corporations, make use of data in running their operations. All the data being used is managed through the use of databases. For this reason, there has been a very high demand for experts in database administration. Being skilled in database development, basically, SQL development proves to be essential.

Data continues to be the central part of numerous mobile applications and web applications. For instance, the Facebook application holds the information of a user's profile as well as data on their posts and friends. To maintain this kind of data, a database system is applied. Therefore, Structured Query Language, is one of the programming languages that allow programmers to work with the available data.

Typically, databases are not designed to understand other programming languages. They know the SQL programming language only. It is a must for those intending to work on app development and web development to learn the SQL programming language. Like all programming languages, SQL possesses its typical markup. Due to this, programmers should find it necessary to be conversant with SQL markup before they can effectively use it in their applications.

Additionally, SQL programming has another unique feature due to its concept of tables. Each database can be presented as a certain number of tables. Every table usually has several rows and columns and acts as a representation of sets of data. The tables allow programmers to store all the information they need.

Several SQL commands are frequently used. Programmers must be familiar with the commands for database work. Some of the commands that a programmers is required to write include:

CREATE DATABASE- This enables the creation of a database

CREATE TABLE- It allows for the creation of tables

SELECT- This is when a programmer finds and extracts data from a database

UPDATE- Helps in making adjustments and editing data

DELETE- It is written when deleting data

Other than the above that are most commonly used, other complicated commands depend on the complexity of the database. It means that the more the complexity of the database, the number of commands the programmer is supposed to use also increases. The commands are used anytime queries are being written. They are referred to as the inquiries that allow programmers to operate the data present in the databases.

In simpler words, when the commands are entered within a database system, they are interpreted and processed by the system. The outcomes are, for instance, new records in the database or new databases are created. In most cases, the initial query is responsible for coming up with a new database.

SQL programming language is categorized into multiple different elements of language; they include:

Clauses- They are the constituent elements of queries and statements. There are instances where provisions are optional.

Expressions- They come up with scalar values or tables that consist of rows and columns holding data.

Predicates- They act as the specifications for conditions that have been evaluated to SQL 3VL (three-valued logic). It can also be in the form of Boolean truth values. They are used in limiting the effects brought about by queries and statements. They are also used in changing the flow of programs.

Queries- They are used when retrieving data based on specified criteria. Queries are essential elements to SQL.

Statements- They have consistent effects on data and schemata. They also control program flow, diagnostics, transactions, sessions and connections. All statements in SQL programming include a semicolon that is a symbol of statement termination. The semicolon is, however, not necessary on each platform. It is one of the standard parts of the SQL language.

Insignificant Whitespace- In most cases it is ignored in SQL queries and statements. This makes it simpler for the formatting of SQL and enhancing the readability of the language.

Inserting, Updating, and Deleting Data

In this section, the topic will be on how to include new records in a database, how to update the existing files, and how to delete the data you no longer need or use. Inserting data is one of the simplest tasks. It is because it starts with simple problems of inserting single rows. In many cases, it is, however, efficient to use set-based approaches when creating new rows. In such a case as a programmer, you will find numerous techniques that can help you insert multiple rows simultaneously.

Similar to inserting, updating and deleting start as simple tasks. A programmer can update a single record and delete a single record. One can as well update multiple files simultaneously using some more sophisticated methods. Similarly, there are numerous ways through which data can be deleted in SQL programming. For instance, one can delete entire rows in a table considering they are existing or not in another table.

SQL also has new additional ways through which programmers can insert, update, and delete data simultaneously. It is one of the best features that SQL programming language can offer.

Inserting New Data

The problem: In this, a programmer wants to add a new record into a given table. In such cases, the programmer uses the INSERT statement when inserting data into tables. The INSERT

31

statement is also referred to as the INSERT INTO statement. It is used when inserting one or multiple rows into tables.

The SQL INSERT statement is used when inserting a single row into a table. Below is an illustration of the INSERT statement used in inserting one row into a table that already exists.

INSERT INTO table (column1, column2...)

VALUES (value1, value1,...)

When inserting a row into a table, a programmer is required to give three specifications. One is the table in which they want to insert the new row, in the INSERT, INTO clause. Second is a list of columns separated by a comma in the table and found within parentheses. The third is a list of values separated by a command surrounded by parentheses inside the values code. The list used for columns should have a similar number of elements as those in the values list. In cases where they fail to match, the SQL database engine will typically issue an error.

An example is using an INSERT statement when inserting new rows into a shipper's table.

INSERT INTO shippers (company name, phone.)

VALUES (Alliance Shippers', 1-680-199-6)

The two constants Alliance Shippers and 1-680-199-6 are identified in the VALUE clause. The SQL engine respectively inserts them into the company name and phone columns. After the execution of the statement, the server in the database brings back a message. That message helps in indicating the number of rows that have been affected. In such a case, the programmers get a message that "1 row affected". This message informs the programmers that there is one new row that has been successfully inserted.

The shipper's ID column is not specified in the column list. This is because the column used for the shipper's ID is an AUTOINCREMENT column. The next sequence is automatically generated by the database engine anytime a new row is inserted into the existing table.

SQL programming provides programmers with a shorter form of using the INSERT Statement to write lesser code.

INSERT INTO table

VALUES (value1, value2,...)

When this form is applied, the list used for values is supposed to have a similar order as the list of columns present in the table. When a programmer uses the INSERT INTO statement, they are required to supply all columns with values apart from the AUTOINCREMENT column. The best thing about practicing the use of column names in INSERT statements is that it helps to make code maintainable.

SQL INSERT statement can also allow programmers to insert multiple rows into an existing table. One can add the rows using one statement.

INSERT INTO table- name (column 1, column2,...)

VALUES (value1, value2 ...)

In such a form, a programmer is required to provide numerous values' lists with each list separated from the other using a comma. Below is an example of an INSERT statement used in inserting two rows into a shippers table.

INSERT INTO shippers (company name, phone number)

VALUES (ALL, 1-400-670-7569')

(DHL', 1-400-522-5435')

SQL INSERT statement also can be used to copy the data table. Other than coming up with specifications of values' lists, a programmer can make use of the SELECT statement in selecting values form other tables and supplying them to the INSERT statement. In such a case, the programmers can easily copy data from one particular table to another.

It is also possible for programmers to block users or delinquent software applications from inserting new values into particular columns in a table. In this case, a programmer comes up with a view on the specific table that exposes only the columns that they wish to unearth. All inserts are then forced to pass through the view. Access is allowed to only users and software that are eligible.

Updating Data in SQL Programming

The SQL UPDATE statement is used in updating the existing data in SQL tables. It is used in changing existing data in a single row or multiple rows present in a table. Below is an illustration of the UPDATE statement.

UPDATE table

SET

　　Column1= new_value1,

　　Column2= new_value2,

WHERE

Condition;

When updating data in a table, a programmer is required first to give a specification of the name of the table that they want to change data in the UPDATE clause. Secondly, include new values for the column that wants to be updated. When a programmer wants to update the data present in numerous columns, every column= value pair and a comma is used when separating the two. Thirdly the programmers should consider specifying the rows that want to be updated in the WHERE clause. The use of WHERE clause is optional and when omitted all the existing rows in a table are updated.

The SQL engines issue messages that specify the number of rows that are affected after the statement is executed. Below are some examples of the SQL UPDATE statements. We can use an example of an employee, Juliet having an id 3, and gets married. The employer is required to adjust the table to be accurate by changing her last name. The existing record name of Juliet may be as follows:

SELECT

Employed, Lastname, first name

FROM

Alliance-ph. Employees

WHERE

EMPLOYEE ID

Employee id last name first name

3 Jolie Juliet

The UPDATE statement will help in changing Juliet's last name from Jolie to Francis

UPDATE employees

SET

   Lastname- Francis

WHERE

   EmployeeID=3

THE select statement is executed to help in verifying the change the will occur as:

Employee id last name first name

3 Francis Juliet

SQL Update Multiple Columns

There are cases where programmers will be required to update data existing in various columns. For instance, in the case of Juliet above, she moves to a new home after getting married. It will mean that the address filled in the original record will change. The UPDATE statement is used in the following way:

UPDATE employees

SET

   Address= '1200 Carter St'

   City= New York

   Postalcode= 4093

Region= CA

WHERE

EmployeeID= 3

Deleting Data from SQL Table

The SQL DELETE statement is used when a programmer wants to delete existing data in a table. To successfully use the SQL DELETE statement, one needs to first come up with the table where the data should be removed in the DELETE FROM clause. Then one should put up conditions within the WHERE clause to help in specifying rows that are to be removed. When the WHERE clause is omitted, every row existing in the table is removed. It is also possible for programmers to delete all rows existing in a table without necessarily deleting the table.

Chapter 5: Modifying And Controlling Tables

Changing Tables

In many cases, SQL database tables that are newly created need to be tweaked a little. For instance, when a programmer is working for someone else, a client may come to them after the database table has already been created and request to keep track of other data items. It means that the programmers will have to return to the drawing board. When one is building databases for their use, some deficiencies in their structures may be quite apparent after the structure is created. For instance, one can get some proposals from different countries and will be required to add county columns. It is the time that a programmer needs to make some modifications to their table.

Simple Modifications to SQL Table Structures

SQL databases are used in storing relationships and data within tables. Changes within the tables are likely to occur from time to time. The changes cater to new or missed out requirements. All SQL tables are structured in ways that they can be modified. Modification of the SQL table structures depends on their complexity; this means that some may be easier than others. Below is a precise analysis of the change of SQL table structures.

All the SQL databases make use of the containers referred to as tables as storage of data and the relationships between these data. There are several rows existing in each table. They are also referred to as tuples where all related data is stored. Each row in an SQL database table usually comprises of columns. These columns are also referred to as fields. Each column stores original data contents. Over time the structure of the table is likely to change. In the case of a business, a supplier ID may need to be increased due to business expansion. Therefore, the number of suppliers may need to improve, and this calls for some changes to the SQL database table structure.

Some of the standard generic modifications that are made to tables include the following.

- Changes to the columns in the table- this can involve changing, adding or removing column types or sizes.

- Changes to constraints and the rules applying to the tables or the relationships among the charts.

- Changing the values of data that are stored in the tables. This can involve, for instance, adding new records, deleting new files or changing the values of documents that are already existing. However, this does not include the modification of the SQL database table structure.

Numerous SQL implementations provide two options that can be used in making modifications within the SQL table. One of the alternatives requires one to use SQL statements. The second option requires one to use GUI tools that are provided by SQL implementation.

Below are some of the steps that one can follow to add new rows and enhance change accommodation successfully. A programmer should open their initial table and follow each step appropriately.

In the window showing table-creation, one should right-click within a small, colored square on the left of the City field. It will help in selecting rows. Then choose Insert Rows from a menu that will pop up. A blank row will appear above the cursor position and will push down every row that exists.

Second, one is required to enter the fields that they want to be added to the existing table. For instance, one can add an Address3 area above the Country and County fields.

The final step is making sure after the modifications are done, the table is saved. This is a crucial step before closing the table. It helps in ensuring that all the changes that have been made are protected as it was required.

The SQL ALTER TABLE statement is used when adding, deleting or modifying existing tables in SQL programming. It is also used in dropping and adding some constraints to SQL existing tables.

The ALTER TABLE- ADD Column is used when adding columns to existing tables. The following syntax is used in the process: it is one of the most straightforward modifications that can be done on current tables. The operation is considered to be free from potential risks. This is because it is not dependent on other elements in the existing database.

ALTER TABLE table_ name

ADD column_name datatype;

When adding an Email column to a "customers" table, the following SQL is used.

ALTER TABLE Customers

ADD Email varchar (255)

ALTER TABLE- DROP COLUMN is used when deleting columns present in a table. There are some databases that do not allow for columns to be removed. For those that would enable, the following syntax is used;

ALTER TABLE table_name

DROP COLUMN column_name;

When deleting an Email column from an existing "customers" table, the following SQL is used.

ALTER TABLE Customers

DROP COLUMN Email;

ALTER TABLE- ALTER/ MODIFY COLUMN is used when making adjustments to the data type existing in a column. The SQL Server/ MS Access is the syntax used in such cases. They are applied in the following manner.

ALTER TABLE table_name

ALTER COLUMN column_ name datatype

Creating some changes in the field structure requires adequate preparation. This is because in cases where the specific field needs some shrinking, essential precautions must be followed. These precautions help in ensuring that data that is already existing in the field is not tampered with as a result of the changes. When numeric field formats are changed, it is possible that inaccuracy or loss of precision can be experienced. In most cases, the SQL systems send some warning if any tampering occurs and the change may not occur if it is affecting the type of data.

Modifying and Removing Constraints

In some databases, there are constraints or rules that are mainly defined for the tables. Therefore, this means that to make successful modifications, one needs to be adequately prepared and make some considerable plans and efforts. This is because in most cases, the adjustments being made are likely to affect the other tables as well.

Dropping columns from existing tables can have some adverse effects on the integrity of the database. This mainly happens when the field being cut is a foreign or primary key of reference by the other tables. The process of dropping the area may be quite challenging. Overcoming it needs a programmer to be adequately prepared and follow all the necessary steps. One should also consider being well conversant with the SQL programming language to ensure they are capable of tackling every task required.

Chapter 6: Working With Subqueries

In SQL programming, a subquery is also referred to as a nested query or an inner query. Subqueries are defined as queries within other SQL queries. They are customarily embedded inside the WHERE clause.

The purpose of subqueries is returning data that will be used in the significant queries as conditions for further restricting of data being retrieved. Subqueries can be completed successfully with proper coordination with SELECT, INSERT, UPDATE, and DELETE statements. They can also be used along with operators such as, IN, =, <=,>=, and BETWEEN.

There are rules that are set to be followed by subqueries. They include;

All subqueries should be enclosed inside parentheses

Each subquery can only contain one column within the SELECT clause. This is possible unless there are many columns existing in the significant query for the subqueries to compare their selected columns.

Subqueries that are returning multiple rows can only be used together with the numerous value operators. Such operators include the IN operator.

The SELECT list must not include any references evaluating to a CLOB, ARRAY, NCLOB, or BLOB.

It is not possible for subqueries to be enclosed in a set of functions.

It is not applicable for the BETWEEN operator to be used with a subquery. It is, however, possible for the BETWEEN operator to be used in a subquery.

In most frequent cases, subqueries are used together with the SELECT statement. There are also instances when the subqueries are used along with the INSERT Statements. The INSERT statements make use of the data returned from the subqueries. This data is used when inserting it into other tables.

Data that is selected in the subqueries is modified using different characters, date, and number functions.

Subqueries are also used in coordination with the UPDATE statements. One or many columns existing in a table are updated by the use of a subquery together with the UPDATE statement. Subqueries are also applicable together with the DELETE statements. In such a case, they are used in deleting records from existing tables that are no longer valuable. When the two are used together, they bring about some changes to the existing table's columns and rows.

There is no specified syntax for use in subqueries. However, in most cases, subqueries are used with the SELECT statements as indicated below.

SELECT column_name

FROM table_name

WHERE column_name

Expression operator

(SELECT COLUMN_ NAME from TABLE NAME WHERE...)

The SQL Server Subquery

It is essential for programmers to understand SQL Server subqueries and how subqueries are used for querying data. SQL servers help in executing whole queries. In the case of customers' tables, it first comes up with lists of customers' IDs. It then comes up with substitution of the identification numbers that are returned by subqueries within the IN operator. It then engages in executing outer queries to help in getting the final outcomes set.

Using subqueries can help programmers join two or more steps together. This is because they allow for the elimination of the need to select the identification numbers of customers and plug them within the outer queries. Additionally, the questions themselves adjust automatically anytime there are changes in the customer's data.

Subqueries can also be nested in other subqueries. SQL programming servers support over 30 levels of nesting. The SQL server subqueries are used in place of expressions. When the subqueries return single values, they are used anywhere expressions are used. SQL server subqueries are used together with the IN operator. Subqueries used with this operator usually returns zero or more value sets. The outer queries make use of the values that have been answered by the central subqueries.

SQL server subqueries are also used with the ANY operator. Subqueries that are introduced using the ANY operators usually have the following syntax:

Scalar_expression

Comparison_operator ANY

(subquery)

When the subqueries return lists of values such as v1, v2, v3, the ANY operator statement usually returns TRUE if there is a comparison of one pair and FALSE when it does not. The ALL operator, on the other hand, returns TRUE in case all the comparisons made pair, and when they do not, it returns FALSE. THE EXIST operators return TRUE when subqueries return results, but when they do not, they return FALSE.

Creating New Databases in SQL Programming

When creating a database in SQL programming, the initial queries are responsible for the creation of new databases. One of the best examples is the Facebook application. The application contains some databases for all the following components.

Users- This is a database on Facebook that is used as a storage for all information on the user's profile. It stores all the details as the person uploads them on their accounts.

Interests- The database on Facebook helps in holding various interests of the user. These interests are applied when tracking down the hobbies and talents of the users.

Geographic Locations- This is a database that holds every city around the universe where any user lives.

The second query when creating a database is responsible for coming up with new tables within specific databases.

Industries That Use SQL Programming

SQL programming databases are commonly applied in technological fields whereby large amounts of data are used. Some of the most common sectors are finance, music applications, and social media platforms industries.

In the finance industries, SQL is mainly used in payments processors, and banking applications. They include Stripe, whereby they operate and store data involving significant financial transactions as well as users. All these processes are supported by complex databases. Banking database systems usually require maximum security. This is, therefore, one of the reasons why the SQL code applied has the highest levels and capabilities of risk compliance.

Some of the music applications such as Pandora and Spotify also require the use of intensive databases. These databases play significant roles because they help the applications to store large libraries consisting of music albums and files. The music stored in there is from different artists. Therefore, these databases are used when finding what users are trying to look for, storing the data about particular users as well as their preferences, and interests.

Social media platforms are other industries that commonly use SQL programming. This is because they require multiple data processing. Some of the social media apps such as Snapchat, Facebook, and Instagram are using SQL to enhance the storage of the profile information of their users. Such information includes biography, location, and interests. SQL is also applied in these applications to improve efficient updating of the application's database anytime a user comes up with some new posts or share some photos. It also allows for the recording of messages that are generally sent from one user to the other. By this, it helps the users to retrieve the messages posted and reread them in the future.

Common SQL Database Systems

The SQL database systems are typically ranked depending on the DB-Engines popularity score. Below are some of the variables that are taken into consideration during the rankings.

The number of times the system has been mentioned on websites. This is measured in terms of the outcomes in queries on the search engines.

The general interest within the system. This considers how frequently it has been searched in Google Trends.

The frequency of technical discussions on the particular database system.

The number of job offers through which the database system has been mentioned.

The number of profiles existing in professional networks whereby the system has been mentioned.

The Relevance of the Database System to Social Networks

1. Oracle Database

This is the most common SQL database system used all over the world today. Numerous industries are using it in their operations. It is, however, commonly used in the processing of online transactions and data warehousing.

2. MYSQL Database

It is one of the open-source database systems in SQL. It is freely available to businesses and individuals. Sit is popularly used by small scale businesses and startups. They commonly use it because it does not have a license fee. It is also used in multiple applications and software programs that are open source in nature.

3. Microsoft SQL Server

The SQL Server is Microsoft's modified database management system. It is used in the running of all main versions of the Windows operating systems. It is also used in the consumer software and web servers running on Windows. This means that the Microsoft SQL server has an extensive user base.

4. POSTGRESQL

It is also a free open source database system. It is commonly used in multiple industries due to free license models.

Chapter 7: Combining Queries

SQL designed to manage relational databases; equally, SQL is used to create queries from the clients' program to the database. You may want to query from more than one table to develop one set of records. You can achieve this through a union query.

However, for one to comprehend union queries, there is a need to understand the basics of designing queries, perhaps in Access or other databases. In the Microsoft office, there is a database that is shipped with Ms. Office suite. You may look for the Northwind Access template to help you understand the basics of designing queries.

After you open the Northwind database, you will be prompted to log in, dismiss the dialog, and expand the navigation pane. For you to be able to organize the database as per their types, proceed by selecting the *Object type*. Next, you will have to expand the Queries group, where you will note a query named *Product Transaction.*

For you to identify the union query, check for a special icon of two intertwined circles. The symbol represents a union of two sets. However, Access graphic queries cannot be united since the tables are not associated with a union query. This is evident when you open union queries from the navigation pane as Ms Access opens it in a datasheet view. In a normal Ms. Access interface, on the home tab, there are two major functions; design view and datasheet view. However, when working with union queries, the datasheet view is not available. Therefore, you can only switch between SQL view and Datasheet view.

For further learning about basic designing of queries, and eventually, how to work with union queries, click the Home function in the Ms. Access interface, then views, and lastly, SQL view to see the SQL syntax that defines that particular union query. Below is an example of SQL syntax of union query as it is in the Northwind database:

SELECT [Product ID], [Order Date], [Company Name], [Transaction], [Quantity]

FROM [Product Orders]

UNION

SELECT [Product ID], [Creation Date], [Company Name], [Transaction], [Quantity]

FROM [Product Purchases]

ORDER BY [Order Date] DESC;

The first and second statements are literally two distinct queries. These queries retrieve distinct sets of records, one fro, *product purchase* table, while the other from the *product order* table. The word UNION between the two statements shows that the two queries will be combined to make them a union query. In the last part of the syntax, the term ORDER BY determines the ordering of the united records. For instance, in this syntax, the abbreviation *DESC* means all records will be ordered by the Order Field in descending order.

How to Create Union Query by Creating and Uniting the Select Queries

It is possible to create union queries by coding the syntax of the union syntax in SQL view. However, it is much easier to develop it in parts with select queries. After developing the independent select queries, you can later copy and paste the SQL parts into the joined union query. Below are the steps of creating a union query by uniting the select queries.

1. In the file menu bar, select create> quires group> query design.

2. Double click the table that has field want to include in the show table. The selected fields will be added to the windows query design window.

3. Now close the *Show Table* dialog box.

4. While in the query design window, double click individual fields to be included in the query. However, ensure to add an equivalent number of fields to each of the select queries, in a similar order. Secondly, ensure the data types in the corresponding fields are compatible with the data you are dealing with and to those of the select queries to be combined with.

5. Although this is an optional step, you may add criteria to the fields by entering the suitable expression in the Criteria row of the particular field.

6. After making sure to have checked all the attributes of the field by checking the data type and, perhaps, adding the field criteria click Design> Results> Run. This will help you to preview the output. Switch the query to the Design view.

7. If the previewed results are as per your wish, save the PostgreSQLselect query.

8. Without closing the windows for the previous select query, repeat the above steps to each of the select queries you wish to combine.

When you are through with creating the select queries, now you will have to combine them to make the union queries. Below are the steps of combining your select queries to form a union query.

1. In the file menu bar, select create> quires group> query design.

2. Close the *Show Table* dialog box.

3. Click Design> query group> union. This will hide the query design window and display the SQL view object option. However, you should note that, at this point, the view object tab will be empty.

4. Select the tab of the first constituent query of the supposed union query.

5. Click home> view> SQL view.

6. Copy the SQL syntax of the select query and paste it in the tab for union query opened in step 3.

7. Each of the select queries has semicolons at the end of the individual syntax, which you should delete.

8. Punch the Enter button on your keyboard to start a new line and type the word UNION.

9. Repeat steps 4 to 8 until you have included all the select queries that you wish to combine. However, DO NOT delete the semicolon of the last select query's syntax.

10. Click Design> Results> Run. This will give you the output of the union query in a datasheet view.

An Example You Can Recreate the Northwind Sample Database

In this example, the union query will collect a combination of names of people from the *Client* table and names of people from the *Distributors* table. Below are the steps to accomplish this task.

1. Start by creating two select queries, Query 1 and Query 2, and name them client and distributor as data sources. Use the First name and Surname field to display the values.

2. Secondly, create another query, Query3, with no data source.

3. Click Design> Union and make the latter query, Query three, into Union query.

4. Finally, copy and paste statements of the selects queries, Qyery1 and Query2, into Query 3. Recall having the semicolon only at the end of the syntax and to add the word UNION between the sentences. You may, at this point, check the preview in the datasheet view.

5. Add to one of the queries in an ordering clause and then paste the ORDER BY statement into the SQL view of the union query. Note that in Query3, when the order is to be appended, the union query first removes the semicolons, then the name of the table from the field names.

6. Your final findings of the combined query should be as follows:

SELECT Clients.company, Clients.[Last Name], Clients.[First Name]

FROM Clients

UNION

SELECT Suppliers.The company, Distributors.[Last Name], Distributors.[First Name]

FROM Distributors

ORDER BY [Last Name], [First Name];

If you are very comfortable writing SQL syntax, you can write your own SQL statement directly to the SQL view for the union query. Nonetheless, using the method of copying and pasting SQL from other database objects, you may find it useful and easier. That request can be much more complex than the simple examples used here for choosing queries. Creating and testing each query carefully before combining them in the union query can be to your advantage. If the union query is not working, you can change each query individually until it is efficient and restore your union query with the corrected syntax.

Chapter 8: SQL Mathematics And Statistics

The basic entities for data science and machine learning are mathematics and statistics. Most of the known and productive data scientists come from one of these areas— informatics, applied mathematics, and statistics, or economics. If you want to excel in data science, you need to have a clear understanding of basic mathematics and statistics.

Nevertheless, studying mathematics can be daunting for people with no interest in mathematics. Next, you need to decide what to study and what not to test. Linear algebra, calculus, probability, statistics, discrete math, regression, optimization, and many more topics can be included in the list.

If you have never been in this field, worry not for this literature will take you through each bit on the same. Here is a list of famous open courses on Coursera, edX, Udemy, and Udacity's data science mathematics. The list was carefully curated to provide you with a standardized path to teach you the necessary mathematics concepts used in data science.

It takes a lot of brainpower and understanding to turn raw and quantitative data into structured and insightful knowledge. It's true that not everyone can be like Aryabhatta, the earliest mathematician; however, you should be strong, concentrated, and committed. With concentration, commitment, and passion in mathematics and statistics, now you just require dedication and hard work to start learning.

Mathematics and statistics are essential disciplines in learning Data Science. Most of the analogies and concepts in Data Science are drawn from the two disciplines. Below is a brief discussion on the different concepts in this field that create data science and its practical uses.

Mathematics and Statistics for Data Science

In today's world, data science has become a phenomenon in engineering. You need to strengthen your knowledge of mathematics and statistics to learn data science.

Mathematics for Data Science

In most of the learning subjects, Mathematics has had much of the domination. The extent to which mathematics is used varies depending on the disciplines. Basically, mathematics can be grouped into two components, namely Linear Algebra and Calculus; these components are part and parcel in Data Science. Below is a brief review of these two fields. In this section you will learn how mathematics contributes to the study of data science.

1. Linear Algebra

Linear algebra is the leading topic in data science. Linear algebra is popular for its recognition of images, text analysis, and also reduction of dimensionality. For instance, can you differentiate a dog from a cat? Yes, you should, of course! The reason being our minds have been conditioned to distinguish dogs from cats since birth. We use our intuition to gain insights into the information as a result.

But what if you need to design an algorithm that can be used to classify cats and dogs? This task is called classification and is a widely used—perhaps the most widely used-machine learning application. As a matter of fact, through linear algebra, the machine can identify the images of cats and dogs.

The use of matrixes is the primary way of storing images. Therefore, linear algebra, which is the most important component of matrices, is highly regarded. Linear Algebra is intended to solve linear equation problems. These equations may contain variables of higher dimensions. It is not possible to imagine or manipulate these higher dimension variables. Therefore, we apply matrix power to help us in manipulating n-dimensional data. Three forms of matrices exist –

- **Vectors** – single-dimensional matrixes.

- **2-Dimensional Matrix** – two-dimensional matrixes; n-rows and n-columns.

- **Scalars** – their order is much greater than two.

Techniques that use Linear Algebra in Data Science

It is essential to note that there are other types of matrices, whose importance cannot be despised, such types include inverse matrix and those of operations such as matrix transposition. Below are the essential techniques used in creating solutions using linear algebra in data science.

Single Value Decomposition – Decomposition of Singular Value helps you to manipulate matrices by separating them into three separate matrices. Scaling, rotating, and shearing of these matrices.

Eigenvalue Decomposition – Decomposition of the original value helps you to simplify the operations of the matrix. This technique is of help in generating new vectors whose direction is identical to the former ones. Further, the matrix is decomposed into eigenvalue and eigenvectors

Principal Component Analysis – They use the Principal Component Analysis to reduce higher dimensions. It is most commonly used to reduce dimensionality, which, literally means, reducing the number of variables or measurements without elimination of correlated tags.

2. Calculus

Calculus is a very important element in data science. Calculus is used primarily in techniques for optimization. It is indisputable that it is close to impossible to learn data science without a primary knowledge of algebra. Calculus enables operations such as performing artificial neural networks, mathematical modeling, and increasing their accuracy and efficiency too. The measurement can be divided into –

2.1. The Differential Calculus

This is the study of the rate of change in the quantity. Derivatives are primarily used to determine the function maxima and minima. Derivatives are applied in techniques of optimization where we need to find the minimum value by minimizing the error function.

Another crucial derivative definition every learner should know about is the partial derivative that is used in neural networks to model back-propagation. Another important concept used to measure back-propagation is chain law. I addition to reducing functions and back-propagation errors, Generative Adversarial Neural Networks differential game theory is applied.

2.2 The Integral Calculus

This refers to the mathematical analysis of quantity accumulation and the field under the curve to be found. Therefore, integrals are classified into certain integrals and indefinite integrals. The operation of integrating is commonly used in calculating functions of probability density and random variable variance. Another important entity that makes use of the integral calculus is the Bayesian Inference.

Upon recognizing the key mathematics subjects, it is equally important to study some of the important data science statistics concepts –

Application of Statistics in Data Science

Statistics refers to the operation of collecting, evaluating, visualizing and interpreting the information. This uses statistics to turn raw data into observations that make up the data goods. The raw data is managed and let companies make careful choices that are guided by data. Statistics provides a variety of resources and features that enable your discovery of tons of data.

In addition, by summarizing and making inferences on data, you can develop a deep understanding of data with statistics. With regard to these two terms, the statistics are separated into two –

- The Descriptive Statistics

- The Inferential Statistics

1. The Descriptive Statistics

To explain the results, descriptive statistics or summary statistics are used. This deals with numerical information analysis. The analysis is achieved by means of diagrams and graphical representations. For one to have a reasonable comprehension of descriptive statistics, it is essential to understand the following concepts:

1.1 Normal Distribution

Here, many data samples are represented in a plot. Equally, there is describing large values of variables in a bell-shaped curve using the normal distribution, also known as a *Gaussian Curve*. The bell curve is symmetrical in nature, expressing that the values are similarly off in both the left and the right directions farther away from the mean taper. For an accurate undertaking of inferential statistics, it is necessary that the data be normally distributed.

1.2 The Central Tendency

Here you identify the central point of the data using a central tendency. Mean, median, and mode are the three primary components of central tendency. Mean is essentially the average of all sample data values. On the other hand, the median is the mid-value of data (arranged in ascending order). Lastly, a mode is the sample's most frequently occurring point.

1.3 The Skewness & Kurtosis

There may be data instances where there is no symmetry in the distribution. A Gaussian curve, for instance, has zero skewness. Whenever data accumulates on the left side, the results are referred to as positive skew, while the contrast implies a negative skew.

The kurtosis tests the graph's "tailedness." From tailedness, we conclude that in either of the graph's tails, kurtosis tests extreme values. Essentially, large-scale kurtosis distributions have tails larger than normal distributions; on the other hand, a negated kurtosis has smaller tails than normal distributions.

1.4 The Variability

As the name suggests, it is the measuring of the distance of the data-point from the central mean of the distribution. However, there are numerous different measures of variability, such as range, variance, standard deviation, and inter-quartile ranges.

2. The Inferential Statistics

It is the process of the data being inferred or concluded. By carrying out multiple tests and deductions from the smaller sample, we draw a conclusion about the larger population by inferential statistics. For example, one may wish to know the approximated number of people who support a certain political party in a survey. The aim is to collect the views of the people, right? However, this method is simply not suitable, because in a country with billions of people, and surveying each of the citizens is a curb some task. As a result, a smaller sample will be taken, and conclusions are made from that sample; thereafter, the findings are attributed to the larger population.

Inferential statistics, there are different methods that are helpful in data science. These methods include—

2.1 The Central Limit Theorem

The mean is equal despite the size of the data; a smaller sample has a mean equal to that of a larger population in a central limit theorem. The actual standard deviation is, therefore, equal to the population standard deviation. The calculation of population means is a vital technique of the Central Limit Theorem. Equally, the margin error is equal to the product of the average standard error and the percentage of trust level z-score.

2.2 The Hypothesis Testing

Hypothesis testing refers to the hypothesis calculation. We assign findings from a smaller sample to a large group using hypothesis testing. We need to test two hypotheses to draw a comparison–the Null Hypothesis and Alternative Hypothesis. The optimal scenario is represented by a null hypothesis; contrarily, an alternative hypothesis typically represents the polar opposite of what are trying to prove correct.

2.3 ANOVA

Checking the hypothesis with multiple groups is done using ANOVA. It is another type of an inferential t-test technique adapted to be more efficient. ANOVA conducts the test with a minimum rate of error. An f-ratio is called a metric for measuring ANOVA. F-ratio is the intergroup mean-square ratio or intergroup mean-square.

2.4 The Qualitative Data Analysis

This type of analysis is made up of two main approaches– correlation and regression. By definition, correlation is the test that involves finding correlations between random variables and bi-variant data. On the other hand, regression is another variation of analyzing qualitative data. In regression, the relationship between the variables is estimated. There are straightforward regression and regression that is multi-variable. Also, we have a non-linear regression if the function is inherently non-linear.

Briefly, the above discussion is on various data science and machine learning computational and numerical criteria.

Therefore, the widespread use of linear algebra in computationally complex tasks has been addressed. Equally, calculus and its use to reduce mathematical models' loss function have been addressed. Additionally, a brief study of how descriptive and inferential statistics are essential in data science was made. Ultimately, we conclude that data science mathematics and statistics are mandatory requirements in data science, for instance, in SQL programming.

Chapter 9: Saving Time With Views, Functions, And Triggers

Arguably, for all business requirements, one strategy is not exclusively the best solution. Therefore, explanations will be made in the next few parts of the key issues to be put into consideration when settling on one solution over another. Often you will find that a combination of methods works best even in a single application.

Best Practices and Approach for One to Achieve a Goal

It is necessary to figure out what you are trying to achieve before choosing one approach over another and then decide how using one approach matches your set objectives. The downside of such a concept is that it gives one a feeling that because it is always right, there is no need to doubt a method. Only follow the best practices outlined in the topic by an expert, and things are going to come into place, eventually. Instead of just focusing on what works best, I would suggest that you think about their primary goal and why one approach is more efficient than another. Therefore, in your consideration, have priorities based on the goal. In this section, we will discuss considerations at a functional level that is very elementary rather than a level of macro applications. Arguably, it is important to view each of an application's operational tasks individually rather than assuming the wholesome of the application. For instance, it may occur that one component of an application that requires the ability to communicate to a mainframe server or run scheduled tasks; however, it is not sensible to drive the entire application structure according to the need for this one-time feature. Therefore, when making your consideration, answer the following questions:

- Does this feature have to work in different database types?

- Is this feature used in several system sections or applications?

- Does this feature require multiple arguments and return one set of values as a single table or as a scalar value?

- Does this feature allow a few arguments to be transferred to the server, but does it require a lot of database information to get results?

- Is the information-intensive or minimal processor function? For example, is it an encryption function or the product of a complex query, or is it more SQL-intensive or more procedural-intensive?

• Are the function parameters consistently the same, or can they be different? For example, a complex search form will not always have to pass the same criteria, but a simple search form will only have one search field and always pass it.

• Is the function page requiring long SQL statements batches, or is it a single line SQL statement?

• Are the result fields always the same or need to be varied? For example, are you always joining the same set of tables that vary slightly depending on the need for different fields or data subsets?

Database Objects

It is very amusing that when people talk about the logic of databases, they tend to focus on stored procedures when, literally, there is almost nothing else. Whether these people have ever interacted with modern systems is still unclear. An original method of encapsulating database logic is stored procedures, but they are not the only method available. Nowadays, most relational databases have views, restrictions, referential integrity with cascading updates, remove, stored functions, triggers, and the like. When used properly, these are strong and effective devices.

The discussion below will cover stored procedures and the other types of database objects in the next couple of sections while describing each of the strengths and weaknesses to encapsulate logic. For each feature 'o', we will assign a score of 0-5, meaning that the feature does not exist, 5 meaning that this is one of the most suitable objects for this type of mission.

Stored Procedures

One of the available methods for encapsulating database logic in the database is through stored procedures. These procedures are similar to regular programming language procedures, which, by arguments, do something, and sometimes return outcomes. However, at times, they even modify the values of the arguments they take when arguments are deemed output parameters. The similarity can be easily drawn considering they can return data; nevertheless, stored procedures cannot be used in queries. Because stored procedures are declared as OUTPUT by the process of taking arguments; therefore, they can return more than one output.

Stored Functions

Except in three major ways, as discussed below, stored functions portray similar attributes to those of stored procedures.

1. These can be used in views, stored procedures, among other stored functions, as opposed to stored procedures.

2. It is prohibited to change data on many servers or have DDL / DML limitations. This is not valid for databases like PostgreSQL, as the distinction between a stored function and a stored procedure is very grey.

3. Generally speaking, they cannot take output arguments (placeholders), which are then passed back with modified values.

Views

Among the function that was received with ululations in the technology field are views. The key advantage of view is that in most cases, it can be used as a table; however, unlike a table, it can perform complex calculations and widely used joints. Except for stored procedures, it can also use practically any object in the database. Views are primarily useful when you are required to enter the same set of tables in order to get overview calculation fields, say an order with an order description.

Triggers and Rules

Triggers are entities usually linked to a table or view that run code based on certain events, such as data initialization before data is added, updated/deleted, and before such events occur.

Triggers can be great things and, at the same time, significantly risky. Triggers are difficult to debug, but strong because the device can easily escape no change to a table with a click.

These are useful for ensuring that certain events often happen while adding or modifying data-e.g. setting complex field default values, inserting record logging into other tables.

Triggers are particularly useful for a particular situation, which is to be applied rather than logic. As we said earlier, for example, most views that include more than one table cannot be modified.

Nevertheless, in Database Management System such as PostgreSQL, you may establish a rule on a view that happens when one attempts to modify or insert it into the view, and rather than inserting, it will occur. The rule can be quite complicated and can set out how, in such a case, the tables should be modified. With INSTEAD OF triggers, MS SQL Server, and SQLite, you are let to do something similar.

Note that the term rule in DBMS is somewhat confusing because it means quite different things.

For example, a rule in Microsoft SQL Server is an obsolete concept used to define tables' constraints. A rule can be compared to a trigger in PostgreSQL except that it is not triggered per row event and is specified without a handling function being needed.

Foreign Key Constraints, Primary Key Constraints, Referential Integrity, Cascade Update/Delete

No constraints, referential integrity, and cascade update/delete, there should be no true repository. Using SQL DDL statements or a relational model, you can describe them. The use of these tools is limited, but with other database objects, the purpose they serve cannot be easily replicated. Two main purposes served by these tools are:

• Provide a database declarative template, and how the data are interrelated, a resource for self-documentation.

• Make sure you are not wrong in your coding to do something dumb to break your pattern. If your design is good, a mistake in your programming logic can signal errors in your code. If you receive errors in your programming logic, test the sound of your template.

Chapter 10: SQL Embedded Java Program

Computers work by utilizing instructions that they receive from people. The different forms of instructions that computers process is called programming. Programming has two essential components: data and explanation of instructions. Computer instructions are written by programmers who apply computer language. There are different kinds of computer languages. For instance, there is Java, Ruby, and HTML. The initials SQL stands for Structured Query Language, which assists in database management. This piece evaluates the various aspects of SQL language, including its brief history, its core elements, and why SQL is embedded with Java program. Additionally, the article highlights and explains some ten common mistakes during SQL programming and how to avoid them. Finally, the article tackles on built-in functions and calculations of SQL.

Overview of SQL

The primary role of SQL is to manage different relational databases and assist in performing different computations on the information. IBM created the SQL program in the 1970s which they called SEQUEL. After sometimes, Microsoft and Oracle started applying for the SEQUEL program. After using the language for sometimes, industry players changed applying the term SEQUEL and started using SQL. One of the fantastic features of the SQL program is the fact that it's an international standardized language that facilitates communication in different databases. This means that this program can permit the implementation of any language like PHP in connection with any particular database including MS Access, MySQL and others.

SQL programming has different features. These include:

1. **High Performance**- SQL programming offers unique and powerful abilities to handle massive databases that are highly used. The programming offers different methods of data analysis and interpretation.

2. **Availability**- SQL programming is friendly to various databases including HANA, MS Access, Microsoft SQL and others. Because most of these databases support SQL programming, it is simple to create additional procedural

functions when they apply the language. This feature makes SQL a powerful programming language.

3. **Scalability**- SQL is highly flexible meaning that you can apply or drop previously formed tables in any database.

4. **Vigorous Transactional Support**- SQL programming enables you to deal with massive records and large transactions.

5. **Data Security**-SQL programming permits access to tables, processes and views. This means that the security of your data is enhanced.

6. **Flexible Applications**-SQL enables programmers to access databases. It's used for both small and big organizations.

7. **Data Management Commands**-SQL programming is applied in different data management systems. The program uses standard commands including select, create, insert, delete and others. These standardized data management commands make the program the best when handling vast amounts of data.

Java Language

Java is one of the well-liked programming languages that is used on different devices. The language is quick, safe and dependable. The java language is object-oriented. The java language is written once but operates anywhere. This means that the Java code is applied in any operating system.

Java language is object-oriented programming that enables the breaking down of a complicated problem into smaller manageable ones by forming objects. Java has different features, including:

1. **Quick**-Although the early versions of java were slug, the current ones are fast. In case you're looking for a fast, object-oriented program, you need to consider java.

2. **Safety**-The language has a variety of features that makes it safe. These include automated memory administration, provision of safe communication by offering privacy and security of information, and the java platforms are secure in creating and operating applications.

3. **Large Standard Library**-Java is a popular program because it has a substantial standard library. The program has different methods and classes that are essential for any developer.

4. **Excellent Performance**- Java is designed to perform highly. The language utilizes bytecodes which are compiled by the compiler. After undergoing the aforementioned procedure, it is passed through a java virtual machine and converted into machine-level code thereafter. All these procedures make the language great.

5. **Object-Oriented**- Java language is completely object-oriented. It has various features that make it a pure object-oriented program. These include polymorphism and abstraction.

6. **Simple to Use**-Java language is simple to learn and understand because of its easy syntax. This makes it the best language for any learner.

Benefits of Java Programming

Java programming has the following advantages:

1. **Simple to Understand**-Java language doesn't have any complications and is simple to learn. In case you're new to computer programming, this is the language to start with.

2. **Performance on Any Network**-Java programming is applicable in any of the operating systems like Linux. The language does not change whenever it's applied in any operating system.

3. **Security**-Java has a highly secure environment where viruses, worms and phishing cannot be condoned.

4. **Reliable**-Reliability is an essential aspect of any computer programming. Java is a trustworthy program because it can detect any problems before its installation. This enables you to collect them on time.

5. **Performance of Multiple Jobs**- Java enables you to perform many tasks at the same time. This is because it's multithreaded computer programming. You can apply it to both pictorial and network programming.

6. **Dynamic**-Java classes are kept in different files and fed into the java interpreter when the occasion demands so. The program can expand its functionality by choosing the classes it needs.

7. **Pocket-friendly**- Java is an open source program. Therefore, you don't need to pay for its license annually. If you want to minimize the costs of operating a business, this is the best programming language to choose.

The SQL Embedded Java Program

An embedded database implies that the database is mixed and cannot be separated from the computer program. Embedding assists in the development of different devices, including mobile phones and specific parts of vehicles. The SQLJ is a program that enables the integration of SQL statements into the java programs. The SQLJ is essential because it allows the confirming of the syntax of SQL statements during conversion.

In ordinary situations, when interacting with Java information, you use JDBC. JDBC is an excellent method when interacting with flexible queries. However, when interacting with static statements, SQLJ is the best approach.

Benefits of SQL

Embedding SQL and java programming has various advantages. These include:

1. **The program is more compact**-this is because it offers a shorter syntax compared to JDBC program.

2. **Error checking**-SQLJ programming is able to detect issues at the beginning and arrest them. JDBC, on the other hand, doesn't check for any mistakes before runtime. Checking errors at the beginning is crucial because it assists the program to avoid them

3. **Comprehensive**- SQLJ program is built to ensure the ease of access of many types of facilities. Examples of these facilities include queries, transaction administration, and others.

4. **Data independence**- SQLJ programming has three ways of ensuring that there is data independence. These include SQLJ is data neutral, the computer programming makes it possible for consortium members to share a familiar translator and the SQLJ code is standard. These features make it possible for an SQLJ to access any database that applies SQLJ.

5. **Vendor-specific customization**- SQLJ programming enables the application of vendor-customization specifications. The program has profiles that are meant to

explain the SQL running. These profiles can be applied in the creation of customized vendor-specific applications. There are two kinds of customizations: profile customization and customization to access specific features.

6. **Flexible deployment**-SQLJ produces a java code which can be applied in any standardized java machine. This enables the natural division of SQLJ programs in different tiers without changing the code.

7. **SQLJ Productivity**-SQLJ can be applied by any professional who is involved in program development. The program is used when dealing with static programming activities. Therefore, the program is relevant to SQL tasks as they're static in nature. SQLJ enables java users to be productivity by applying SQL programming and avoiding data programming.

8. **Brevity of commands**- SQLJ commands are brief when compared with JDBC.

Disadvantages of SQLJ Programming

1. **Requires a pre-processing step**-this makes waste the time of a programming developer.

2. **Some IDEs lack SQLJ support**-this can be a stumbling block for programmers who want to apply for the program.

3. **Oracle 12.2**-it does not support SQLJ in its database.

Requirements for SQLJ

Before applying SQLJ, you require the following:

1. **SQLJ Translator**-this converts SQLJ files into java.

2. **Java compiler**-the java compiler should be friendly with JDK.

3. **SQLJ runtime classes**-the SQLJ has different packages like sqlj.runtime.

Development Goals of SQLJ

SQLJ computer programming was developed by Oracle. The program aims are as follows:

1. **Accessibility of static data**-SQL is static data. Therefore, the developer of SQLJ wanted to build a program that allows the accessibility of the static data.

2. **Independence of semantics and syntax locations**-this is because the two features do not rely on the configuration in which the program operates.

3. **Group of vendors**-This SQLJ programming supports specific groups of vendors. The vendors are willing to embrace the program's support.

Chapter 11: Common Rookie Mistakes

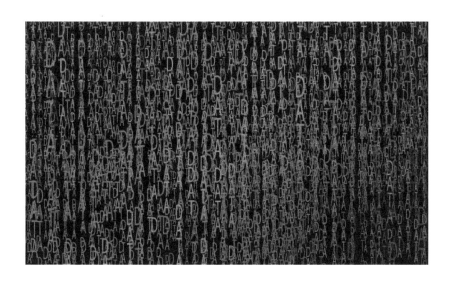

Although SQL is a simple computer programming language, you may find it hard when working with massive data. It is essential to ensure that you write high-quality statements before you start working on moderate and huge tables. As you engage in writing your statements for various sites, you need to avoid the following mistakes:

1. **Primary Keys**-Primary keys are essential when working with each of the SQL tables. The primary keys are used to identify rows in a table. You'll not produce impressive work without the keys. The primary role of these keys is to quicken queries. Having the primary key should be the first step when handling relational databases. It's

essential to ensure that you apply a primary key in all the tables that you form.

2. **Repetition of Data-**Repetition of the same set of data in different tables is referred to as data redundancy. It's essential to ensure that each table has different kinds of data set and avoid repeating it. In order to make sure you don't repeat the same data in different tables, it crucial that you abide by normalization rules. If you repeat, you create confusion. For instance, you may have a table that has a client's mobile number. Since the mobile number belongs to the client, it can quickly identify them. It'll be wrong to create an order table and add the client's mobile number again. To avoid this mistake, it's essential to store your data in a single location and apply relationships existing between the primary and foreign key in handling your data.

3. **Use Join-** Many programmers commit a mistake of applying statements that are poorly optimized. It's essential to desist from using statements like: NOT IN and IN. Although these statements are convenient, you can easily avoid them and apply JOIN instead. Using JOIN ensures that your data is optimized.

4. **Forgotten NULL vs Empty String Value-**You have the choice of either using the NULL or apply actual values

like nil. However, it's vital to ensure that you retain uniformity in the database.

5. **The asterisk character in SELECT statements-**To ensure that there is standard performance and safety; you must define and identify the sections that you need to return when querying.

6. **Avoid Using Too Many Cursors-** Use of too many cursors when performing your SQL is bothersome. It's essential to desist from applying too many loops when undertaking your SQL procedures. Although loops are a common feature in programming, they're ineffective in SQL. Instead of using them, you can apply effectively presented SQL statements. In case you occasionally use cursors, it's important to minimize them.

7. **Data Mismatches-**Upon establishing your table columns, it's crucial to provide a data type to all of them. The data type must contain all the information that you need to keep there. The definition you give to each table column should guide you in determining the info that you need to store therein. For instance, table columns that are meant to store decimal information should not be used to store integers. In case you store a different set of data in a column instead of the one defined, you may mess up your database. At the outset, it's essential to determine what

you want to store in each table column ensure that you actually keep it as defined.

8. **Using of AND and OR operations**-Sometimes, you may fail to adhere to a logical order when writing your queries. The way you apply the AND and OR statements may change your information. It's essential to apply the right parenthetical structures or arrange your statements in the right pre-determined sequence.

9. **Selection of Wrong Database**-Upon establishing your SQL, it is crucial to choose the right database from the window. To avoid this mistake, you must always check the database that you've.

10. **Spelling Mistakes**-SQL is a machine language and may be harsh if you misspell the words. For instance, instead of typing the word SELECT you write SELCT. You need to desist from making this mistake by ensuring that you type the words correctly using capital letters. You also need to create borders that separate your main words from other words and table columns.

11. **Missing Brackets and Single Quotes**-These grammatical structures are applied many times in SQL programming. They come in pairs. The errors that many people make is that they either forget using these structures or don't apply them properly. For instance, you

may use an opening bracket {(} and forget the closing one {)}. SQL also requires that you enclose text figures in single quotes. In case you don't have a quote, SQL may not understand where your text starts and stops. To stop committing these mistakes, it's essential to remember that brackets and quotes come in pairs and always observe this rule when dealing in them.

12. **Commas and Semi Colons**-These punctuation marks are applied in SQL for different purposes. Whereas commas are used when separating lists, semi-colons are applied to signal to end of an expression. To avoid these mistakes, ensure that you place a comma in the front. Semi-colons are optional and may or may not be used.

13. **Failure to Review Your Data Model**-The data model that you build determines how the users access your information. It's essential to think of the kind of model that you require and the simplicity with which your users access it. Failing to determine the model that you need attracts complicated queries and complex codes as you progress with your work. To avoid these mistakes, it's essential to have a printout of the data model that you want. You can also invest in a data modelling tool that can help you. When you use either a printout or a modelling tool, you determine what you might not want in your database and avoid it on time.

14. **Failing to Determine the Right Logic**-You've two kinds of logic when performing your SQL: cursor and set-based logic. You need to determine the best form of logic which satisfy your needs.

15. **Discarding Old Techniques**-Some programmers avoid applying old techniques because they think that they're no longer helpful. In case you want to avoid any unnecessary errors, it's essential to apply the old tested and tried techniques. Avoid rushing to embrace new tactics that you lack much information concerning them.

16. **Avoiding Peer Review**-Consulting a knowledgeable person to review your query plan is essential before you deploy it. The reviewer may discover some few things that may have escaped your attention. You'll also benefit from the suggestions and comments of the reviewer.

17. **Failing to Test Queries**-Many developers avoid testing their queries due to a variety of reasons. For instance, they claim that testing is thorough and may not have the time to do so. However, it's essential to acknowledge that testing is a vital process in coding. You need to ensure that you have rigorously tested your code and it apes the final production environment.

18. **Not Minding Your Syntax**-Syntax means the way words come together to form phrases and sentences

thereafter. In case you don't arrange your words well, you'll not make a sensible statement. Likewise, in case you don't apply the right syntax your database may not understand what you're saying. This may result in poor performance.

19. **Assuming That Your Clients Understand What They Need**-When clients call you, do not assume that they fully understand their database problem. It's essential to let them know that you're a professional in that area and you'll assist them in discovering the problem and fixing it.

20. **Project Scope**-Some rookie SQL programmers fail to demand an adequately documented project scope from the clients. Due to this mistake, clients keep adding more tasks on top of the first ones that make the work enormous but poorly paid. Before you embark on any SQL project, it is essential to ensure that you sign a contract that captures all the tasks that you're required to offer. Any additional task that is not captured in the contract must attract an additional payment.

21. **Nontechnical Aspects of The Project**- Before you commence any SQL writing project, it's vital to consider other nontechnical factors that may impact on how the project is delivered. Factors like politics and business environment may have any impact on the way the SQL

project is delivered. You need to enlighten yourself on some of these factors before you start delivering it.

22. **Avoiding Feedback**- Although you'll be inclined to listen more to the managers who offered you the job; it's equally important to listen to the end-users of the program. So, apart from listening to managers, it's also important to listen to the users of the program like the clerks.

23. **Reviews**-Some rookie programmers may avoid selecting a professional reviewer to offer them essential suggestions about the program design. Before you begin the project, you need to identify a reviewer who can provide helpful tips on how to improve it.

Chapter 12: Built-In Functions & Calculations

In regard to SQL, a built-in function can be defined as a portion of programming that accepts zero or any other input and returns an answer. There are different roles of built-in functions. These include the performance of calculations, obtaining of the system value, and application in textual data manipulation. This part aims at examining the various SQL built-in functions, categories of functions, pros and cons of functions and types of built-in functions.

Types of SQL Functions

The SQL functions are grouped into two groups: aggregate and scalar function. Working on Group by, the aggregate functions run on different records and deliver a summary. Scalar functions, on the other hand, run on different records independently.

These are as follows:

1. **Single Row Functions**-They provide a one-row return for any queried table. They are found in select lists, START WIH, WHERE CLAUSE and others. Examples of single-row functions include numeric_, data_mining, Datetime_, conversion_ and XML_functions.

2. **Aggregate Function**-When you apply this kind of function, you see a single row returns based on different rows. The aggregate function exists in Select lists, ORDER BY and HAVING CLAUSE. They go hand in hand with Group by Clause and SELECT statements. Many of them do not take attention to null values. Those that are usually used include AVG, EANK, MIN, SUM and others.

3. **Analytic Function**-They are used to compute an aggregate value that are found on specific groups of rows. When you run this function, it delivers many rows for every group. The analytic functions are the last one to be run in a query. Examples of analytic functions include analytic-_clause and Order-by-Clause.

4.   **Model Functions**-These are found in SELECT statements. Examples of model functions include CV, present and previous.

5.   **User-Defined Function**-They are used in PL/SQL to offer functions that are not found in SQL. They mostly used in sections where expressions occur. For instance, you can find them in select list of Select statement.

6.   **SQL COUNT Function**-It is used to provide the number of rows in a table.

Categories of Functions

Functions are classified according to the role they play on the SQL database. The following are some of the function categories available:

1. **Aggregate Functions**-They do a calculation on a specific set of values and deliver a single value. The aggregate values are used in the SELECT LIST and HAVING clause. The aggregate functions are referred to as being deterministic. This means that they return the same value when running on the same input value.

2. **Analytic Function**-They calculate an aggregate value according to a group of rows. They return many rows for different groups. The analytic functions can be used to perform

different computations like running totals, percentages and others.

3. Ranking Functions-They provide a ranking value for each portioned row. These kinds of functions are regarded as nondeterministic.

4. Rowset Functions- They're used to return an object that can be applied.

5. Scalar Functions-They work on a single value to return the same. There are various kinds of scalar values. These include configuration function, conversion function and others.

a) Configuration Functions-They offer information about the present configuration.

b) Conversion Functions-They support data changing.

c) Cursor Functions-They provide information concerning cursors.

d) Date and Time Data Type-They are concerned with operations as regards date and time.

6. Function Determinism-Functions that are found in SQL servers are either deterministic or nondeterministic. Deterministic functions provide the same answers when they are used. Nondeterministic functions, on the other hand, offer different results when they are applied.

SQL Calculations

There are various mathematical functions build-in the SQL server. The functions can be classified into 4 main groups, including Scientific and Trig Functions, rounding functions, signs and random numbers. Although there are numerous mathematical functions within each class, not all of them are used regularly. The various classes are highlighted and explained below:

1. Scientific and Trig Functions-Under this category, there are various subclasses found under it. These include P1, SQRT, and SQUARE. P1 function is used to compute the circumference and area in circles. How it works: *SELECT 2 *10.* SQRT connotes square root. This function is used most of the time. The function recognizes any number that can be changed to float datatype. Example: *SELECT SQET (36) Returns 6.*SQUARE means that you multiply any number by itself. The concept of Pythagoras theorem is useful here. This means that **A**squared+**B**squared=**C**squared. This can be performed as **SELECT SQRT (SQUARE (A) + SQUARE(B)) as C.**

2. **Rounding Functions-** Under this class, there are various subcategories which include the CEILING and FLOOR. The ceiling function is helpful when dealing with a float or decimal number. Your interest is to find out the highest or lowest integer. Whereas the CEILING is the best highest integer, the floor represents the lowest integer. The ROUND function is

applied when you want to round a number to the nearest specific decimal place. This is expressed as ROUND (**value, number of decimal places**).

3. **Signs-** There are occasions that require that you obtain an absolute figure of a number. For instance, the absolute value of -7 is 7. The absolute number doesn't contain any sign. To assist you with this task, it's essential to utilize the ABS function.

4. **COS (X)-**This function recognizes an angle expressed as radian as the parameter. After an operation, you get a cosine value.

5. **SIN (X)-**This function notices a radian angle. After computation, it gives back a sine value.

6. **Sign-**You can use a sign function when you want a negative, positive, or zero value.

The Importance of SQL Built-In Functions and Mathematical Applications

The build-in functions are sub-programs that help users to achieve different results when handling SQL database. These applications are used several times when you want to manipulate or process data. The SQL functions provide tools that are applied when creating, processing, and manipulating data. The benefits of SQL in-build and maths functions are as follows:

1. Manipulation of Data-The in-built tools and maths functions play a significant role in data manipulation. Manipulating massive data may be difficult if you do it manually. This is especially when the data is massive. Therefore, these functions play a significant role in ensuring that your data is manipulated fast as per your demands.

2. Assist in The Processing of Data-To benefit from data; you must process it. You may never have the ability to process big data manually. Therefore, the built-in SQL functions and maths applications assist you in processing your database.

3. Simplifies Tasks-In case you're a programmers, you can attest to the fact that these functions and formulas make your work ease. You can work fast when you apply these in-build functions and formulas. Due to these tools, you'll accomplish many projects within a short time.

4. Increase Your Productivity-Using the in-built functions enhance your productivity as a programmers. This is because the functions enable you to work quickly on different projects. In case you were to handle data manually, you may take much time before you accomplish a task which ultimately injures your productivity. However, the built-in functions and calculations allow quick execution of tasks.

5. Time Saving-Because functions are written once and used several times, and they save much time. Besides timesaving, the functions offer support to modular programming.

6. They Enhance Performance- When you apply functions; you enhance the performance of your database. This is because the functions are prepared and inserted prior to usage.

7. Enhances Understanding of Complicated Logic- Handling of SQL database is a complex tax. Therefore, functions enable you to decompose data into smooth and manageable functions. In this way, you find it easy to maintain your database.

8. Cost Effective-Because the functions are in-build in the SQL database; you can use them many times without the need to invest in new ones. In this connection, therefore, they reduce the cost of operating and maintaining your SQL database.

Downsides of In-Built Functions

The SQL in-built functions have various limitations, including:

1. **Testability**- When using the in-built functions, it's challenging to test their business philosophy. This is a big challenge, especially when you want the functions to support your business philosophy. You may never understand whether the functions are in line with your business vision and mission.

2. **Versioning**-It's challenging to establish the kind of version that is used in the SQL build-functions. You need to understand whether there're any new versions that can probably provide the best service.

3. **Errors**-In case there are errors within the in-build functions which you don't know, they may disrupt the program. This may prove costly and time-wasting.

4. **Fear of Change**-In case there is change; you may not understand how it will affect your SQL built-in functions. The world of technology keeps changes, and this change may affect the in-built functions.

The SQL in-built functions and calculations are essential as they enable a programmer to execute a task fast with minimal errors. The calculations in the in-built database makes it possible to process and manipulate data.

Chapter 13: SQL Joins

This chapter seeks to inform you about SQL joins their fundamentals as well as a sneak preview of how you can handle them. When you are analyzing data on the SQL platform, you will sometimes need to work on several tables and merge them to achieve the set goals. The skill of joining or merging tables is essential for data scientists, even though some scientists don't take it seriously. This chapter will enlighten you about the various types of table joins and how you can be able to apply them to SQL.

We will start by discussing the basic concepts of SQL joins and later look at the various types of joins in existence today. This chapter ends with a quick look at different types of queries applied when using more than one table. To understand this topic, you should have beginners' knowledge of SQL and writing a simple question in the PostgreSQL.

How to Setup the Database Environment in SQL

You need to create a few tables for your analysis before studying the basics of joins. The most recommended kind of table is one having at least one column. You can, however, implement the join queries on similar tables without necessarily creating a new one.

A tool is known as pgAdmin that comes up when you install PostgresSQL helps you perform almost all SQL operations. It is a tool that can be created on a database to create tables in a case where you won't have a database in existence. The following specifications can help you create tables, check them out.

name_student (the name or id) student_stream (student id)

You ought to note that the two tables share a common column. To build a table, you can apply a create statement to create those tables. The table entries ought to have a clean outline if you followed the table creation instructions. At the end of it, you should have at least two simple tables for this discussion. Having learned that, we next discuss the fundamentals of the SQL joins.

Basics of SQL Joins

The joins will let you collate or merge more than one table with the use of primary identifiers. To understand this, let us look at the two tables we created earlier: all of them share and an id column. You might be wondering what the purpose of joining in SQL is? Well, we discuss that next.

Given the constraints associated with normalization, you might miss out on some of the vital information in one table. The process of normalization isn't only recommended but also a must to ensure consistency, bring down redundancy levels as well as preventing various insertions and updating issues. Let's go back to the two tables again, suppose you want to locate the stream in which a student named Sayak has been enrolled. To do so, you will have to merge the tables and then carry on accordingly.

For you two to join two tables, they must be an everyday thing between those two tables. How can this be achieved? Having the two tables share a column with the same name? Or what does that statement exactly mean? Well, we discuss this next!

The tables that are supposed to be joined might not share a column that has the same name, but in a real sense, the two tables should have a common name. For instance, each set of data should have a thing in common. In this case, you cannot merge two or more tables that have a column with a similar name but with a completely different set of data types.

To break this down further, we next discuss the various types of Joins in SQL.

Types of SQL Joins

This part of the chapter discusses the different types of joins in SQL joins. We shall discuss each participates to have a clear understanding. It is recommended you first visually study the joins and later execute the set join queries as highlighted in SQL.

The Inner Join

It is one of the most popular types of joins in SQL. For you to understand it better, take another look at the two tables we created earlier. In those tables, the column we are putting under consideration is the one with ID details. In columns where values aren't common in either of the tables, inner join ignores the rest of that column. Below is am executed example of a query where the inner join is performed in between both tables. These are the student name and the student stream. Once you have completed the question is indicated below, you will attain the exact results as presented in the table.

The self-join option lets you carry out the joining process on the same table, saving you the time you spend organizing the final table. There are, however, a few situations where this can be a good option. Imagine the chart you created earlier has the columns consisting of country and continent.

When faced with a task of listing countries located in the same continent, a clearly outlined set below should give you a glimpse of the results expected.

The Outer Join

This type of SQL join can further be subdivided into three different types: the left join, the right join as well as the full outer join. The outer join primary role is returning all the identified rows from a single table, and once they join the target is archived, it includes the columns from another table. Outer joins are different from inner joins in the essence that an inner join cannot involve the unmatched rows in the final set of results.

When using an order entry, for instance, you may be faced with situations where it is inevitable to list every employee regardless of the location, they put customer orders. In such a case, this kind of joins is beneficial. When you opt to use this kind of join, all employees, including those that have been given marching orders, will be included in the final result.

Let us discuss the three types of outer joins we highlighted earlier.

The Left Outer Join: This is a kind of outer join that is responsible for returning each row from the first left side of the table and those row that match from the right side of the table. In case there are no matches on the right side, left join returns a null value for each of those columns.

The Right Outer Join: It is a type of outer join that is tasked with returning each row from the right side of the table and those that merge from the other side (left) of the table. Again, if there aren't any values for those digits in the column, the join returns null values for them.

The full outer join: it is tasked with returning rows from their initial location in the inner join, and in case there is no match found, this join returns null results for those tables.

The Cross Join

It is a kind of join that is essentially a product of cartesian elements that is expressed in the SQL set up. Picture this; you require a whole set of combinations available between both tables and even in just one table. You will have to use the cross join to achieve that technique. To help you understand this join better, you can go back to the two tables we created at the beginning of the article. Look at both the columns and try to compare the impact each one of them has to the final result. The cross join plays an essential in ensuring accuracy during merging. You ought to note that there are apparent differences between cross joins and outer joins, even though the description makes them almost look similar. We hope to discuss that in this chapter as well.

Some scientists have questioned the need to combine data with the SQL joins. Well, this has sparked a heated debate on whether it is essential to do. We shall briefly look at why it is vital to combine your data with SQL joins. To better understand this, let's look at other forms of SQL and how they function. SQLite and various databases like the Microsoft SQL servers related in some way. These databases have made it easier for you to build data tables as well as a faculty to link the data closer together.

Given the requirements needed to achieve a set of indicated goals, the joins are aligned against basic practices to reduce data quality problems. This is done through a process known as normalization, which enables each table to attain a particular meaning and goal. Picture this, you have a table containing various columns with each having crucial information, and you want to change just a section of it; this can be very difficult if you don't have a recommended recovery mechanism in place.

Chapter 14: Ten Tips For Easy Retrieval

In this chapter, we will discuss some of the best tips you can retrieve SQL. To begin with, we need to understand what SQL select is: this refers to a kind of tool that helps you in digging up hidden info in a particular database. It does not matter whether you know what you want to retrieve, being able to translate that idea to SQL can be a difficult task. You need to be very careful with it because even the slightest mistakes will lead to wrong results. To help you stay on track, we have highlighted the following then tips on avoiding the errors.

1. Verifying Database Structures

When you succeed in retrieving data from your database, and it ends up not making logical sense, you should check the design of your database. It could be because a lot of the databases are poorly designed; if this is the case, you will have to first fix that design before working on another solution. You should keep in mind that good design is essential data integrity.

Most database administrators, as well as developers, mostly assigned character data types on columns that have specifically numeric data. The digital data columns contain any data and are better with catch-all.

2. Querying on the Test Database

This tip can be implemented by creating a test database containing a similar structure as that of the production database, but this time, only with a few elements representing it in the table. Select data so as you can foretell the kind of results the queries will portray. Additionally, you should deploy every query test on your data and establish whether the outcome matches your expectations. In case they do not match, you will be forced to restructure your queries. Again, when you reformulate your questions and still end up with the wrong outcomes, you may be forced into your entire database.

Create various sets of data sets, and just for accuracy, you should include uncommon cases like the empty tables as well as ridiculous values that fall far off the allowable costs. Picture scenarios that are unlikely to happen and check out for complete behavioral changes in case they happen. In the process of doing so, you are more like to picture out what kind of problems might occur, and well, you will be better prepared.

3. Confirming the Queries that Contain Joins

Joins are known to be commonly counterintuitive. In case the query you are working on has one of the mentioned joins, you must ensure that it is performing according to how you instructed it before adding it where other clauses are located. The other thing you ought to do is avoid assigning too much memory.

You ought to know that as part of the administration and installation of SQL, it allows indicating the level of memory assigned to the SQL servers. However, you should know that allocating too much mind to the SQL servers will increase the weight on general servers by preventing it from essential memory resources that can be used to perform other tasks like operating systems and apps.

This trick is also very appropriate, especially with databases that have been inactive for quite some time. Some other retrieval techniques can be useful as well, but not as accurate as this can be. Follow the steps we highlighted carefully and watch your data set get retrieved.

4. Confirm the Queries that have Subselects

Queries that contain subselects can obtain data from a table and based on the kind of data that has been retrieved, it might interfere with the set data in a different schedule. From this, we can tell that recovering such type of data can be so hard. You should ensure that the kind of data the inner join retrieves is the same that outer select requires to output desired results. You need to be even more careful in cases where you have more than one level of subselect.

You should also avoid using highly duplicate telexes. This is because a highly duplicated index has a limited set of unique values. To understand this better, let us look at the following example. Imagine you have highlighted an index on the set column which contains slightly less than three values, it means the index is a highly duplicated value. What most people don't know is that having a highly duplicate set of the index isn't good compared to not having it at all. This is because when indexes are highly duplicate, it will force the engine database to work harder to process it during very critical operations like updating or deleting data.

5. Summarize Your Data with GROUP BY

Picture this; you are working on a table that consists of data about the national baseball league. It can contain information such as the name of the player, teams playing in the league as well as the number of first runs scored by each baseball player in the league. You can be able to retrieve the total points for the home team with the following query. Select team, Add (the home team from nation league group by team): This query will display a list of the total number of home teams, the goals scored as wells the players who scored them. In a majority of identified implementations, such kind of a query can result in null outcomes or errors. In the previous types of data retrieval methods, we have seen more of using data sets that are aligned in columns, than those aligned in rows. There are different ways you can apply that set by using a particular set of formulas. This segment has discussed two methods that, when used appropriately, can result in the desired outcome.

6. Analyze GROUP BY Section Restrictions

Let us assume that you need a table that consists of the league's top goal scorers. The following query will help you come up with your target results.

SELECT Player, Team they play for, Home Country they come from >= 25 GROUP BY Players:

In a standard set up, this query will result in an error. However, this shouldn't mean that it is not a performing retrieval method. Generally, in this method, the selected columns applied in the grouping or the columns involved in a user query are more likely to appear in that particular list. In q situation where you will prefer viewing that set of data, use the following collection of functions.

SELECT Player, Team they play for, Home Country they come from >= 25 GROUP BY Players:

Because the columns you would like to display in clause appear to be named GROUP BY, it successfully delivers the results you objected to and desired. This is achieved through enlisting the name of the team, then players, and lastly, the total number of goals scored by each player.

7. Apply the Parentheses with Clauses NOT, OR & AND

In some situations, when a scientist mixes the clauses AND & OR, SQL will mostly won't carry out the expression in the manner you expected to or how you planned. It is therefore recommended that you include these parentheses in the set of sophisticated expressions so that you can ensure you attain your desired results. Keying in an extra set of critical strokes will ensure you smaller reparation for the error you made, and in return, more accurate results.

This set of parentheses will ensure that each game of the clause is applied in the keyword or term you instructed it to. This ensures not only a more accurate set of information but also consistency.

From the previous methods of retrieval, this can be said to be among the most affordable of them all. It does not require complicated steps or technicians to do it; contrary, you only need basic knowledge to pull it through. Most scientists have recommended it for the efficiency and accuracy that comes with it. Try using it and watch out for improved, efficient, and more accurate results!

8. Regulate the Retrieval Privileges

Most of us do not take advantage of the security apparatus that are available in the DBMS. They are not ready to be involved with them because often, they think that misusing and misunderstanding of data are things that only happen to inexperienced people.

However, this is not true; I advise you to establish a significant security device in your system and maintain it so that you can have a more secure set of information. In other words, this segment is encouraging you to ensure that you maximize the security apparatus available in your system.

Additionally, do not hesitate to summarize all the instructions your data set has identified. Even though many have not approved this retrieval method, it is one of the most efficient, and I would advise you to go for it!

A study done by a leading company in Chicago revealed that this retrieval method is safer and does not expose your data to any theft or vulnerability. As we said earlier, this method is also safe and affordable.

9. Regularly Back up your Databases

Most people think that data is challenging to retrieve when a power outage occurs during infernos, earthquakes, or any other natural disaster that can destroy your hard drive. You should also keep in mind that sometimes, a computer can die on its own, without warning and with your essential information. It is advisable to back up your data frequently to avoid these inconveniences, store the backup media in a secure location.

What do we mean by a secure location? Well, this will depend on how crucial your data is and its importance. It can be anywhere: a fireproof section of your house, it can be a few blocks from where your computer is, or a concrete bunker dug under the mountain and modified by hardening it to without horror scenes like nuclear attacks. It is, therefore, in your hands to decide the kind of security you want to accord your data set. It doesn't matter how weak it can be; the bottom line is ensuring your data is backed up somewhere safe.

10. Handling the Error Conditions Effectively

Whether you are developing a set of queries around your workstation or applying questions to a particular app, many times, the SQL will return error feedback or something you did not expect. In such situations, it essential to decide the next step to undertake, depending on the kind of message that was returned.

In applications, however, the situation is usually a little bit different. The application user is not generally aware of the appropriate action to take. To take care of such uncertainties, you are advised to install an extensive error handling software into your system. It will effectively tackle every error that might occur. You should, however, note that creating an error managing code needs a lot of effort. It is one of the most complicated procedures that will require you to be a little more careful. The result of it is worth it. Give it a try and watch your data get secured!

Chapter 15: Stored Routines And Variables

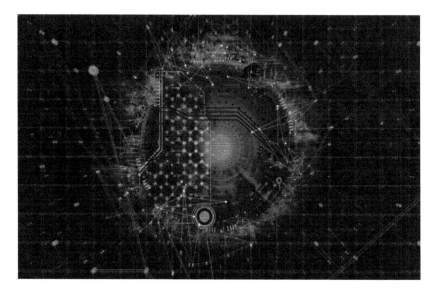

This chapter discusses the variables in a stored procedure and how you can declare them and use them as well. Additionally, we will also discuss the various scopes that the variables contain.

Let us begin by defining a variable. Well, a variable refers to a named data object that its value is not constant and can change during stored procedure fulfillment. In such occurrences, you can use the procedures that have been saved to maintain instant outcomes. These kinds of results or variables are essential to the method you have stored. You should be aware that before you use any variable, you must declare it first.

Declaring the Variables

To declare a variable, you are recommended you use the following 'declare' statement. Declare variable_user, the data method (measure) [Default default_type]:

In that connection, you must first begin with specifying the name of each variable immediately after you announce a keyword. You must ensure that the name of your variable follows the naming regulations of MySQL column names.

Secondly, you need to ensure that you have specified the data length and type of variables you plan to use. There are different sets of data types that variables can contain, such as Datetime, INT, and VARCHAR. Some of us might be wondering what they mean. To break it down further, you ought to know that these variables refer to the basic sets of rules you use when filling up a table. To this point, we have discussed a host of regulations that are necessary to come up with when working towards achieving your desired goals.

Thirdly, you tasked with assigning a set of variables a primary value through the default option. An amount is certified null when you declare its variable without identifying a default value. The MySQL data set enables you to denote more than one set of variables that have a standard collection of data using the statement we identified earlier on. You can use the following collection of data to declare a variable that contains a similar data set.

Similarly, MySQL system has a slot that allows you to announce more than one set of variables that have a standard type of data. Again, most of the technicians have had issues with how this command relays information to related databases. In the various methods of storing variances and variables, this one has proven to be more secure than others. Consequently, it has been known to be the most popular of them all.

Variables can be applied in mathematical expressions, for example, adding values altogether or combining and holding texts. It can be applied as a section of the general information. For your information, variables are employed in storing information so as one can participate in a kind of calculations. Additionally, variables can be part of the parameters and are used in procedural assessments. It is a two in one method that not only lets you declare a variable but also setting it up with values that have a similar data type. When remembering the examples we gave earlier, we can affirm that varchar is a kind of data that lets you sustain more than one kind of character in just a single string.

At this point, you should be in a position to understand the kind of data sets and various types in existence. This knowledge will not only let you be in an excellent place to tackle errors in case they occur and prevent them from happening as well. When Hillary Bladiwn, a renown data scientist and a graduate of Oxford University, first used varchar, he recommended it for being efficient and accurate. He rated it among the best types of data set in the market today. It does not have an allocation for potential occurrences of errors. It is hard to interfere with such a highly secure kind of data type.

The self-variable option lets you carry out the joining process on the same table, saving you the time you spend organizing the final table. There are, however, a few situations where this can be a good option. Imagine the chart you created earlier has the columns consisting of country and continent.

When faced with a task of listing countries that located on the same continent, a clearly outlined set below should give you a glimpse of the results expected.

This type of SQL variable can be subdivided further into three different types: the left join, the right join as well as the full outer join. The outer join primary role is returning all the identified rows from a single table, and once the joining target is archived, it includes the columns from another table. Outer joins are different from inner joins in the essence that an inner join cannot involve the unmatched rows in the final set of results.

When using an order entry, for instance, you may be faced with situations where it is inevitable to list every employee regardless of the location, they put customer orders. In such a case, this kind of joins is beneficial. When you opt to use this kind of join, all employees, including those that have marching orders, will be included in the final result.

Let us discuss the three types of variables we highlighted earlier.

This is a kind of outer join responsible for returning each row from the initial left side of the table and those row that match from the right side of the table. In case there are no matches on the right side, left join returns a null value for each of those columns. A type of outer join is tasked with merging each row from the right side of the table to the other side (left). Again, if there aren't any values for those digits in the column, the join returns null values for them.

It has the task of returning rows from their initial location in the inner join, and in case there is no match found, this join returns null results for those tables.

It is a kind of variable that is essentially a product of cartesian elements that have been expressed in the SQL set up. Picture this; you require a whole set of combinations available between both tables and even in just one table. You will have to use the cross join to achieve that technique. To help you understand this join better, you can go back to the two tables we created at the beginning of the article. Look at both the columns and try to compare the impact each one of them has to the final result. The cross join plays an essential in ensuring accuracy during merging. You ought to note that there are apparent differences between cross joins and outer joins, even though the description makes them almost look similar. We hope to discuss that in this chapter as well.

Chapter 16: Exercises, Projects And Applications

SQL in full is the Structured Query Language and is a kind of ANSI computer language that has been specially designed to access, manipulate, and update database systems. SQL has different uses; the most significant of them is managing data in database systems that can store data in table forms. Additionally, SQL statements have been used regularly in updating and retrieving data from databases.

What we have thought since childhood is the best to learn a new concept is by practicing it. It is no exception; you have to do various equations related to SQL as a way of learning about them. This section seeks to provide you with a list of exercises or equations that when you solve them, you will be in a position to resolve your issues related to this topic. Check them out!

Examples of Exercises in SQL

The following are random exercises that you can do in SQL. Assuming you are an employee of a particular research company and you have the task of finding out data about customers in a specific business establishment. Below are some of the queries you are more likely to encounter.

- You are instructed to construct a query that can display every customer that has spent over 100 dollars in a hotel. This exercise will help you acquire mathematical skills in SQL.

- Draft down queries that will indicate every customer that resides in New York City and has to spend over two hundred dollars in the business establishment.

- Draft down questions that will show every customer that either live in New York City OR has spent over two hundred dollars in the business establishment.

- Draft down queries that will indicate every customer that either resides in New York City or HAS NOT to spend over two hundred dollars in the business establishment.

- Draft down queries that will indicate every customer that DOES NOT reside in New York City and HAS NOT to spend over two hundred dollars in the business establishment.

- Draft down queries that will indicate either the orders NOT issued by the last day of the week by a salesman whose identification number is 505 and below and the rules that the amount spent on them is one thousand dollars and below.

- Write down a SQL equation or statement that displays the salesman's identification number, his name, and the city that he comes from. Also, ensure that the commission involved has a range of more than 0.20%, but below 0.15% captured.

-Draft a SQL query that shows every order that customers spend no more than two hundred dollars on, don't include those that were made passed the tenth of February, and purchased by customers that have identification numbers below 5009.

- Pen down SQL statements to isolate the rows that fulfill the orders made before first August, and the amount spent on them is below one thousand dollars. Secondly, let it include the customer identification numbers that are more than one thousand.

- Draft a list of SQL queries that will display the order number, the amount of money spent, the number of targets achieved, and those that have not been made. Also, indicate the name of the salesman working on them and their success rates.

Projects in SQL Programming

Below are random projects that you can encounter in SQL programming. They have been picked and randomly, and I believe if you practice them out, you will be better equipped in handling such situations. Before we list the projects, we first should get to understand the differences between exercises and projects. Well, logically, a task is more of a quick test you can do without a lot of complications: it is less complicated compared to projects. On the other hand, projects are a little more complicated and sophisticated. It requires advanced skills as well as data research to do it.

Having learned that, let's discuss the potential projects you can encounter in SQL programming

i) Interviews

When making software for a particular company, you will need knowledge of an existing system that belongs to that company. For such purposes, you will have to carry out interviews for some individuals working in that company and collect critical information. You will have to do interviews on people that are aware of that software. Such people could be working as hostel wardens or trainers.

ii) Discussions (Groups)

They can be a kind of group discussion that has occurred between employees of the company you are working on. For a start, a good number of ideas might appear clustered together or filled by concepts that already exist. Such ideologies might be brought on board by programmers.

Additionally, it can be done through online observation. It is a procedure of obtaining more essential details about the existing software or web apps from the web. The primary purpose of this project is getting as close as possible to the system. SQL programming plays a critical role in ensuring the systems are up and running as recommended.

Applications of SQL

The self-variable option lets you carry out the joining process on the same table, saving you the time you spend organizing the final table. There are, however, a few situations where this can be a good option. Imagine the chart you created earlier has the columns consisting of country and continent.

When faced with a task of listing countries located on the same continent, a clearly outlined set below should give you a glimpse of the results expected. SQL variable can further be subdivided into three different types: the left join, the right join as well as the full outer join. The outer join primary role is returning all the identified rows from a single table, and once the joining target is archived, it includes the columns from another table. Outer joins are different from inner joins in the essence that an inner join cannot involve the unmatched rows in the final set of results.

When using an order entry, for instance, you may be faced with situations where it is inevitable to list every employee regardless of the location, they put customer orders. In such a case, this kind of joins is beneficial. When you opt to use this kind of join, all employees, including those that have been given marching orders, will be included in the final result.

This is a kind of outer join that is responsible for returning each row from the first left side of the table and those row that match from the right side of the table. In case there are no matches on the right side, left join returns a null value for each of those columns. A type of outer join has the task of returning each row from the right side of the table and merging with the other side (left) of the table. Again, if there aren't any values for those digits in the column, the join returns null values for them.

It has the task of returning rows from their initial location in the inner join, and in case there is no match found, this join returns null results for those tables.

This is a kind of variable that is essentially a product of Cartesian elements that have been expressed in the SQL set up. Picture this; you require a whole set of combinations available between both tables and even in just one meal. You will have to use the cross join to achieve that technique. To help you understand this join better, you can go back to the two tables we created at the beginning of the article. Look at both the columns and try to compare the impact each one of them has to the final result. The cross join plays an essential in ensuring accuracy during merging. You ought to note that there are apparent differences between cross joins and outer joins despite the fact that the description makes them almost look similar. We hope to discuss that in this chapter as well.

Similarly, MySQL system has a slot that allows you to announce more than one set of variables that has a common type of data. Again, most of the technicians have had issues with how this command relays information to related databases. In the various methods of storing variances and variables, this one has proven to be more secure than others. Consequently, it has been known to be the most popular of them all.

Variables can be applied in mathematical expressions, for example, adding values altogether or combining and holding texts. This can be used as a section of the general information. For your information, variables are also applied in storing information so as one can participate in a kind of calculations. Additionally, variables can be part of the parameters and are used in procedural assessments. This is two in one method that not only lets you declare a variable but also setting it up with values that have a similar data type. Going back to the examples we gave earlier, we can affirm that varchar is a kind of data that lets you sustain more than one kind of character in just a single string.

Up to this point, you should be in a position to understand the kind of SQL Exercises and Programs as well as the various types in existence. This will not only let you be in an excellent place to tackle errors in case they occur and prevent them from happening as well. When Mark Suaman, a renown data scientist and a graduate of Havard University, first used varchar, he recommended it for being efficient and accurate. He rated it among the best types of data set in the market today. It does not have an allocation for potential occurrences of errors. It is hard to interfere with such a highly secure kind of data type.

Since its introduction in the computing world, SQL has played a significant role in revolutionizing data storage in a systematic manner as well as direct retrieval. As the digital world continues to grow steadily, the amount of data stored quickly escalates, making organizations and personal data piling up. Therefore, SQL acts as a platform where these data are stored while offering direct access without the emergence of limitations. As such, SQL is used in different sectors, including telecommunication, finance, trade, manufacturing, institutional, and transport. Its presence primarily deals with data but also accompanies other significant benefits on its application.

Data Integration

Across the sectors mentioned above, one of its main applications of SQL is the creation of data integration scripts commonly done by administrators and developers. SQL databases comprise of several tables which may contain different data. When these data are integrated, it creates a new experience essential for the provision of meaningful information, therefore, increasing productivity. Data integration scripts are crucial in any given organization, including the government, as it offers trusted data which can be utilized to promote the achievement of the set goals.

Analytical Queries

Data analysts regularly utilize Structured Query Language to smoothen their operations more so when establishing and executing queries. That is, as discussed earlier, SQL comprises multiple tables that consist of different datasets. When these data are combined, it brings out more comprehensive information critical for any individual or organization. The same is also applicable for data analysts as they use a similar aspect. As they use an analytical query structure, queries, and tables from SQL are fed into the structure to deliver crucial results from varying sources. In this case, data analysts can readily acquire different queries and customize them to have a more comprehensive data to depend on as solutions.

Data Retrieval

This is another important application of SQL to retrieve data from different subsets within a database with big data. This is essential in financial sectors and analytics as to the use of numerical values typically consists of mixed statistical data. The most commonly used SQL elements are create, select, delete, and update, among others. The technique is made possible when the user quickly can search the database and acquire the needed data as SQL sieves the information to bring out the desired data. In some cases, the language may deliver similar or related data when the required data is missing. This is crucial as one can compare the results as well as make changes where the need arises.

Conclusion

As mentioned above, SQL is used in different sectors globally and applied in different areas to help in data management. One of them includes index structures modifications that encompass the creation of pathways that helps in the collection of data that quickly trace information of interest. SQL can also be applied as a technique to modify and change database tables. That is, it helps in keeping the data stored up to date, therefore, eliminating instances of outdated data, which are often misleading.

www.ingramcontent.com/pod-product-compliance
Lightning Source LLC
LaVergne TN
LVHW051243050326
832903LV00028B/2550